Praise for *How to Dungeon Mas* ͏͏͏͏͏ͅ

"A must-read for any Dungeons & Dragons fan ready to take on the most dangerous adventure of all: parenting. Equal parts funny and practical, *How to Dungeon Master Parenting* is like a core rulebook for raising kids. I wish I had this kind of advice before my wife and I started our own party of adventurers."—**James Breakwell,** author, *Only Dead on the Inside: A Parent's Guide to Surviving the Zombie Apocalypse*

"As a parent and D&D fanatic, everything about this book resonates with me. Shelly brings her humor, warmth, and infectious energy into every page, making this not only a useful parenting guide but a dang fun read! A must-buy for any D&D-inclined parent!"—**Michael Witwer,** *New York Times* bestselling author

"In this funny and relatable book, Shelly Mazzanoble proves that parenting is the ultimate adventure—challenging your endurance, strength, and ability to deal with unexpected challenges. I'm just disappointed there aren't more sleep spells to help out at bedtime. This book is the perfect gift for the D&D-loving parent in your life." —**Julie Vick,** author, *Babies Don't Make Small Talk (So Why Should I?): The Introvert's Guide to Surviving Parenthood*

"Mazzanoble has created the ultimate manual for RPG-loving parents hoping to maneuver the magic and mayhem of raising little monsters of their own. A critical hit for any grown-up geek aspiring to conquer parenthood!" —**Aaron Reynolds,** author, *Fart Quest*

"*How to Dungeon Master Parenting* is an engaging book that offers relatable advice for parents who enjoy tabletop roleplaying games. Shelly Mazzanoble's friendly and nonjudgmental tone creates a welcoming atmosphere for new parents, making it a great read for those about to embark on their own parenting adventure. The book provides practical guidance and helpful tips, along with relatable anecdotes and humor to help parents navigate the challenges of parenting with a smile. You will even find the stat blocks and legendary actions for your small human! Shelly invites you to the adventure of parenting by showing you how to use your skills as a player and Dungeon Master to help you multi-class into parenting. This book does a good job of showing how one parenting style will not fit all and how to have a sense of humor as you adapt and learn how to best work with your own children. A must-read for all soon-to-be parents!"—**Dr. Megan Connell**

"Make no mistake about it, parenting is a quest. With barbarian meltdowns, monster naps, and mimic emotions, it can be tough to navigate that quest. Shelly's book gives parents a new way to approach parenting. Now we are Dungeon Masters and adventurers. Told with a delightful and fun voice, the book contains actionable and specific advice that will help any parent dungeon crawl through the darkest odyssey."—**Shannon Carpenter,** author, *The Ultimate Stay-at-Home Dad*

"Who knew a book on parenting would make me a better Dungeon Master . . . or wait . . . a book on Dungeon Mastering would make me a better parent? Whichever it is, Shelly's book is an insightful, pithy guide filled to the brim with stories and gems on how to be the best parent/DM you can be. Your quest is to figure out if it goes on the game shelf or in the nursery. Enjoy!"
—**Todd Stashwick,** actor/writer/Dad/DM

"The epic-level handbook of parenting is finally here! As a friend, fellow parent, and seasoned Dungeon Master, I can verify that this book is filled with laughter, sage advice, and practical tips that transform raising your kids into an epic quest. A must-read for all parent adventurers out there!"—**B. Dave Walters,** author, *Dungeons & Dragons: A Darkened Wish*

"Shelly knows that storytelling and collaboration is the real magic behind D&D, and it comes through on every page. A vibrant new generation of DMs and players will find a lot to love here as they embark on new adventures together."
—**Jim Zub,** author, *Dungeons & Dragons Young Adventurer's Guides Series*

How to
Dungeon Master
Parenting

How to Dungeon Master Parenting

A Guidebook for
Gamifying the Child-Rearing Quest,
Leveling Up Your Skills,
and Raising Future Adventurers

Shelly Mazzanoble

UNIVERSITY OF IOWA PRESS | IOWA CITY

University of Iowa Press, Iowa City 52242
Copyright © 2024 by Shelly Mazzanoble
uipress.uiowa.edu

ISBN 978-1-60938-981-9 (pbk)
ISBN 978-1-60938-982-6 (ebk)

Printed in the United States of America

Cover design by Amanda Hudson
Text design and typesetting by April Leidig

Printed on acid-free paper

Cataloging-in-Publication data is on file with the
Library of Congress.

For Quinn, the boy who made me a mom,
and Bart, the guy who made me want to be a mom

Contents

Prologue: Session Zero Clue

My mom always said, "Babies don't come with rulebooks," which likely accounts for why so many parenting books are sold every year. *How do you turn this thing off?* Sorry, you can't. They don't come with on/off switches either.

My mom also said, "Choose your battles. You don't have to fight all of them!" She probably meant it's okay to let your kid go to school in mismatched socks or stop trolling that know-it-all mom in the neighborhood Facebook group who waxes on about the best organic corn nuts, but I like to imagine she was a savvy Dungeon Master skilled in steering a Dungeons & Dragons adventuring party toward clever puzzles and malleable monsters easily defeated with Charisma-based ability checks. Babies, and their future selves, are formidable Big Bad Evil Guys and Gals (BBEGs), but with the right knowledge and tools they can be tamed. As gamers know, everything is more fun when you gamify it, and parenting is no exception. You can have almost as much fun bringing up a baby as you can rolling up a character.

Wait, what's this about Dungeons & Dragons? Who is this Dungeon Master? Are we talking about another highly contested parenting style meant to counteract the effects of gentle parenting? And should babies really be allowed in dungeons? I might be new to this and all, but even I know infants are much too young to appreciate spelunking. Besides, stalagmites are definitely a tripping hazard. Or is it stalactites? I still get confused. In any case, allow me to step back. If you don't play Dungeon & Dragons, you probably missed the word "Dungeon" on the cover of this book and are either very confused or very disappointed right now. Don't worry. Even if you've never contemplated the effects of the Deck of Many Things or held the iconic twenty-sided die in your palms, Dungeon Masters (DMs) can help you too! Maybe you've read stories about how D&D enriches the lives of its players and provides numerous benefits like fostering community, encouraging creative and critical thinking, boosting confidence, forging friendships, igniting the imagination, and providing the much-needed social connection the world feels like it's still catching up on. Therapists use D&D in their practices, teachers use it in the classroom, and even industry powerhouses from tech to entertainment credit the game with helping to hone their creativity and the crucial interpersonal skills needed to become effective leaders. Coincidentally, these are all qualities necessary to thrive in the often unpredictable, sometimes terrifying world of parenthood. If D&D can make you a better person, couldn't it make you a better parent too? That got me thinking. What if parenting *was* a game—or at least inspired by one? As senior brand manager for Dungeons & Dragons; cohost of *Dragon Talk*, the official D&D podcast; and mother of a son on the cusp of his tween years, thinking about gaming and parenting isn't exactly new to me. What if the core tenets of the World's Greatest Roleplaying Game could be applied to raising a child and help parents and parents-to-be master or, rather, *Dungeon* Master parenting? I'm no parenting expert (ask my kid), nor am I a professional Dungeon Master (ask my players), but I am the favorite parent 65 percent of the time. Plus, four out of six of the kids I Dungeon Mastered for said they'd play again. (They didn't specify with *whom*, but I'm known for handing out candy and office swag, so I'm making some assumptions here.)

I've spent five days a week for almost twenty-five years around some of the greatest people I have ever known. It's the nature of the job, or at least *my* job. They are dedicated, compassionate leaders who make you feel like a hero. They speak with authority yet foster an atmosphere of autonomy. They're creative, empathetic, and collaborative. They're not afraid of rules: some they follow, some they make, and some they break if it means a better experience. They make mistakes, sure, and graciously own up to them. Failure is full of opportunities. They root for your success and celebrate your victories. They know how to manage different personalities and how to bring disparate groups together and fight for a common goal. They are cheerleaders and task-bringers. They make challenges fun. They inspire and ignite. And they never stop working. They're not always parents, but they are always Dungeon Masters.

Without Dungeon Masters, we players would be out-of-work adventurers with cool backstories and half-drunk potions, wondering how we all know each other. DMs prepare the framework for our collective story, bring out the hero in all of us, and keep everything from grinding to a halt when the party decides they don't want to take the job and would rather sit in a tavern all day wondering if the barkeep looks a little shady. Their mere presence at a table signifies good times ahead. I have no idea where we're going, but my rucksack is packed, and I already ate half of the rations.

Being a Dungeon Master is like playing Whac-a-Mole with the prefrontal cortex of the brain. You don't get into this role without the best of intentions. It's a huge undertaking. You *really* want to do a good job. You spend days planning and plotting. Poring over sourcebooks and getting lost in Reddit threads about how to give your nonplayer characters (NPCs) personality. You calculate the distance from Winterhaven Forest to the Blacklustre town center by foot *and* horse-drawn carriage. If your adventurers are thirsty and want to purchase a pint of Dwarven ale from a local brewer, you know exactly how much it costs (1 sp) and maybe even (most definitely) created your own label for it.

And for what do you ask in return? Well, as Bret Michaels, the distinguished librettist of the 1980s glam rock band Poison, once sang, "Don't need nothing but a good time."

I think Bret speaks for all Dungeon Masters. Aren't we all just after a good time? Every decision, every dice roll, every graphite line carefully laid out on paper or monster token placed on a virtual tabletop is just another bullet pinging the universe's armor, trying to manifest social affirmation and memorable moments. Every D&D game should end with stronger bonds, excited players clearing their schedules in anticipation for the next session, and a proud Dungeon Master absolutely beaming. We really should be celebrating these people more.

Sure, DMs can prepare for a game by drawing maps, designing complex encounters rife with puzzles and traps, and bookmarking monsters from the *Monster Manual*, but can they really anticipate the players' moves and motivations? Of course not! There is no way to know how fascinating the NPC staffing a booth in an open-air market will become, but next thing they know, they're spending the next two hours spinning tales about "Scurvy, purveyor of the Sword Coast's most delicious tangerines" from the small farming town of Mierskar. Meanwhile, the pathway leading to a secret goblin mining town remains untrod, and they have another distinct voice to remember. Those Dungeon Masters must remain nimble. They relish the unexpected! And if they panic, they never let you see it. It's all about ad-libbing and flexibility, the "Yes, and . . ." rule from improv, and 100 percent faking it until you make it.

You can take the Dungeon Master out of the game, but the game stays with the DM. And that's a good thing! By its very nature, D&D fosters the aforementioned skills, and no one embodies them more than our beloved Dungeon Masters. Do you have to buy all the core rulebooks and learn how to be a DM before your child arrives? Absolutely not. (But I'm not going to stop you if you really want to.) Do you need to go to South America to learn how black lion tamarins use tree sap to self-medicate? No, you google it like everyone else. Like the researchers in Brazil's Atlantic Forest, I have intensively studied our game-playing subjects and am here to report my findings. Besides, you probably have your hands full trying to figure out how to assemble a travel crib or come up with a name to attach to this tiny human that doesn't rhyme with a bodily function or remind your partner of some kid from middle school they still hold a grudge against. (RIP "Karen" and "Chad." Who saw that coming?) Fortunately, DMs are excellent teachers who are used to being observed in the wild. All you need to do is *embody* the essence of a Dungeon Master. It's a game of roleplaying and make-believe, after all.

My early research corroborated my "good Dungeon Master equals good parent" theory, which was great news because I had already written the book proposal and three chapters. I, like Bret Michaels, am also looking for a good time, but parenting is more than just a fun pastime. (That whole "fear of ruining someone's life" sure is a buzzkill.) I fully recognize everything you're about to read is largely inspired by my own experience as a married, white, straight, cisgendered woman. I'm also really terrified of babies and teenagers, which is going to factor in. The beautiful thing about parenting is that no one's experience—like the kids you're raising—fits perfectly into a box. It's all subjective. The same can be said about D&D. Diversity isn't just celebrated; it's encouraged. No two wizards are the same. They learn different spells, come from different backgrounds, have different chips on their shoulder from a Lord of Waterdeep who *absolutely* knew there were doppelgangers running that town and yet told the party you were just trying to retrieve a stupid heirloom! While the paths we took to parenting and the makeup of our families may not look the same, there is plenty of common ground in this world filled with elves, owlbears, and magic. We are united in this quest to raise the next generation of heroes.

Parenting has even more "rules" than Dungeons & Dragons, and the ones holding the most reverence apply to both.

- **Rules are for chumps.** Or rather, stressing about rules is for chumps. It takes time to settle into your role either as DM or parent and figure out it's you who gets to have authority over the rules. There are no "official" parenting rules, and the ones that fill thousands of pages in D&D books are there to be a guide. Use only what feels right for you and your family (and of course ones meant to keep you all safe; it's much harder to find a healing potion in the real world). Think of parenting as your own home-brew campaign.

- **It's supposed to be fun.** A game is fun, but what's fun about a *baby*? Admittedly babies aren't getting a Las Vegas residency anytime soon, but they can be entertaining. The whole seeing the world through a child's eyes sounds like a creepy warlock spell, but it is pretty magical. I remember watching my toddler son discover the joy of falling leaves. To an adult with a yard, you might think, *Ugh, what a nuisance! Gotta rake these up.* But to a human who's only been a person for eighteen months, a pile of red and gold yard waste is an enchanted, mystical playground. Parenting isn't *exactly* a game, but it's also not supposed to feel like a table-read for a psychological horror. (Again, no one told the babies that and some of them are advanced in the method acting arts.) The important thing is to keep your sense of humor. If you can't laugh your way through a massive blowout as you're about to board an airplane, your baby isn't going to be the only thing that stinks.

- **Get an adventuring party.** In game, these are your fellow heroes who you will work with to achieve your common goals. In real life these are your fellow heroes who you will work with to achieve your common goal. Huh. More alike than I thought. Your IRL party can be your partner, your family, a network of other parents, or even your actual D&D party. You have a much better chance of success if you support each other and work toward your common goal—hopefully goals you discussed before this baby drops onto your lap. (Also, babies don't drop onto laps, sadly, but you'll need a different book if you're confused about that.) Remember all those clichés like "There's safety in numbers" and "Misery loves company"? They were written about parenting.

Looks like my mom was wrong—finally! There *is* a guide for raising children—the *Dungeon Master's Guide*. Clearly gamers love reading rulebooks, so why not give them a rulebook for parenting? "Play" is how children learn best, and now the same can be true for you too. Warm up your dice. We're going on an adventure.

Moppet Manual: Shrieking Enchanter

It's not cool to rifle through the Dungeon Master's secret notebook to find out what threats await your heroes. And yes, all DMs have secret notebooks. Peeking at it is a major party foul. Don't do it. Besides, who do you think you're fooling showing up to an umber hulk fight with your *cloudkill* spell ready to go? Everyone knows your wizard never prepares that one.

But soon-to-be parents don't like surprises, which is why gender reveal parties are even a thing. Again, you can't be totally prepared for what your child is going to throw at you (and I mean that literally, because you're going to spend the next twelve years bobbing and weaving everything from projectile vomit to dirty basketball socks), but you can be prepped with basic survival knowledge. In this case, it's not just okay to sneak a peek at your enemy's stat blocks; it's encouraged.

The *Monster Manual* is the preeminent bestiary for Dungeons & Dragons. It contains a menagerie of iconic creatures and beasts inspired by folklore, mythology, and, in the case of the Rust Monster, a cheap plastic toy. Incidentally you can do a fun social experiment with the *Monster Manual*. Put it within six feet of a child, and if they are drawn to it, you are looking at a future Dungeon Master. Like moths to a flaming sphere, baby! The book defines "monster" as "any creature that can be interacted with and potentially fought and killed." Good lord, we're not talking about the latter, but "interacted with and potentially fought" is most definitely in your future.

Your ~~monster~~ (Editor's Note: Shelly, please stop referring to children as monsters. You're scaring the new parents), er, child will progress through many stages, leveling up in strength and abilities, and presenting a host of new challenges. It's almost like they shapeshift into a new creature right before your eyes. You too will gain experience with each standoff. Whether it serves you in the next inevitable matchup or gets tossed into the "things we'll never try again no matter how desperate we get" column remains to be seen. But you *will* level up, even if you must claw your sinking body out of a pool of rice cereal to get there.

Armor up, meet your first fearsome opponent, and grab your luckiest set of dice.

Shrieking Enchanters are wily beasts. These nocturnal nightmares appear innocent and helpless, which is how they draw in their humanoid prey. Acting as if they are in need of 24/7 protection, Shrieking Enchanters flash a chubby thigh or issue a soft, lilting coo, reducing intelligent humanoids of sound mind and body within a hundred-foot radius to hired rodeo clowns who can only communicate

SHRIEKING ENCHANTER
Tiny fey, Chaotic Neutral

Armor Class 4
Hit Points more than you think
Speed 0 ft

STR	DEX	CON	INT	WIS	CHA
4	0	1	2	1	22

Skills Deception +4, Persuasion +3, Performance +6
Senses Blindsight 60 ft, passive Perception 12
Languages Crying, Grunting, Shrieking
Condition Immunities charmed, exhaustion, grappled, paralyzed, petrified, restrained
Challenge 12 (17,000 XP)

Eject Goo. Shrieking Enchanters create an endless supply of gooey substances, which spew spontaneously from various orifices. Goo targets any creature it can see within 8 inches. The target must make a DC 25 Dexterity saving throw. On a failure, the target takes 55 points of acid damage and is stunned until it changes its clothes.

Innate Spellcaster. Shrieking Enchanters have innate spellcasting, allowing them to cast the following spells at will: *charm person, fear,* and *cloudkill.*

Burrito Hold. They are immune to *sleep* spells but can be placated if they are wrapped up like a burrito and placed on their backs.

ACTIONS

Claws. Even though their fingers are teeny tiny, their fingernails grow at an accelerated pace and will continue to grow until someone musters the courage to trim them. *Melee Weapon Attack:* +12 to hit, 1 target. *Hit:* 15 slashing damage.

Noxious Odor. The Shrieking Enchanter emits a noxious gas in a 30-foot cone. Each creature in that area must succeed on a DC 18 Constitution saving throw or become paralyzed or poisoned.

in high-pitched, singsongy voices. The Shrieking Enchanter did not come here to make friends and is not impressed with silly games (unless it's the one where you repeatedly hold something up to cover your face and then quickly reveal your face; that one is *comedy gold*). All opponents have disadvantage on saving throws against *charm* spells.

These fearsome fey babes are unpredictable and irrational. A high Charisma score is wasted on them. They throw off their opponents by constantly changing their likes, dislikes, wants, needs, and entire personality, appearing helpless and humble one day and inconsolable and irritable the next. Sometimes all of the aforementioned in the same hour. In melee, a Shrieking Enchanter will resort to reckless flailing or spewing bodily fluids all over their opponents. They are attracted to shiny, pretty things like dry-clean-only clothing, jewelry, and human hair.

No, that is not a smile, it is definitely gas. You better run.

➤ **Best Defense:** *Catnap.*

Parenting at 1st Level

So, a funny thing happened about ten years ago. Bart, my husband, and I discovered our adventuring party was going to increase by one. Normally that's a good thing. A cleric with a soothing healing word? A tricky rogue with an eye for trapdoors? A badass paladin with a pure heart and bludgeoning mace? Yes, please, the job is yours! But our party addition wasn't protective, clever, or badass. In fact, they weren't going to contribute much to our party at all except another thing to fret about and a whole lot of equipment to carry. With the right outfit, maybe they'd get a Charisma bonus.

Starting a family is a joyful, exciting, and terrifying time for parents-to-be. I suppose some people spend more time in the joyful or excitement camp, while others are neck-deep in terror, paralyzed by doubt and paranoia. (It's me. I'm "others.") I blame the Prep for Baby 101 hospital classes I signed up for, believing they would do just what the course name promised. *Prep for a baby.* Pretty sure "questioning all your life choices" was unintended extra credit. These classes were basically the D&D core rulebooks for new parents, except imagine the core rulebooks weren't designed for a game of make-believe and instead prepped you for real-life monsters and other horrors you were absolutely going to face. (So, kind of like what those Satanic panic zealots from the eighties believed was happening.) Look, no one is more aware of their own shortcomings when it comes to child-rearing than I am. I didn't even know a lot of babies. *By choice.* Before my own kid, the only time I was responsible for a child was when I was twelve and my mom negotiated a babysitting deal for my former babysitter's two-year-old. How cute, right? The sitter surpasses the sitter. Except I didn't. Not even close. Why would anyone leave a twelve-year-old with zero experience and an acrimonious-at-best relationship to young children in charge of a toddler? I spent more time watching MTV than watching their sweet daughter, but our time was formative because it was there, in little Abby's living room, where I first saw Bon Jovi's "You Give Love a Bad Name" video. I was so mesmerized by Jon Bon Jovi's magnificent perm and beautifully applied eyeliner, I didn't notice little Abby creating her own work of art on the sofa with . . . let's just say an *organic medium.* I was not asked back the following summer.

Maybe it was because I didn't spend a lot of time around them, but I didn't even really like kids. When my friends announced their pregnancies, I sighed and rolled my eyes and counted down the months before they inevitably traded me in for a mom they met at their prenatal yoga class. Off I went to Marshalls to purchase another soft stuffed bunny and cute pair of shoes I had no idea would be impossible to put on a baby, never mind totally impractical. Their feet seldom hit the ground! Why did they need shoes? When my cousin's son was left alone with my child-free adult cousin and me, he (clearly able to read the room) asked where his mom was and we told him a dingo ate her. We thought nothing of it. It was the natural response two childless grown women would give a small child asking for his mom, right? Just rolled off the tongue. We resumed our cackling and wine drinking, until the aunties converged on us and demanded to know why we thought it was *funny* or *appropriate* to terrorize a *baby*. First of all, he wasn't a *baby*. Babies wore diapers and didn't have the capacity to ask questions like "What did you witches do to my mommy?" This kid had to be at least three and a half. (He was two.) Second, how were we supposed to know that kid didn't have a fully developed sophisticated sense of humor like we did. Jeez. Sorry if I failed to memorize all the developmental milestones. Other than a love of naps and Goldfish crackers, what did I even have in common with kids? Obviously, I had a lot to learn, which is how Bart and I ended up in the deluxe classes for dummies. Hopefully this portal to progenitorship included lessons like "Don't tell babies their moms have been eaten by wild doggies because kids are very literal."

Key takeaway: Force anyone even *considering* parenthood to take these classes, because it's too late once you're expecting! Bart and I viewed these courses like mini quests, each granting us enough experience to level up our nonexistent parenting skills. However, each class left us feeling like we were starring in a *Scared Straight* video. These classes were not led by Dungeon Masters. They were led by powerful mages who wore sandals and caftans cut just low enough to see the giant unakite crystals dangling from their necks. The lanyards carrying their freshly printed ID badges were covered in buttons with pithy sayings like "Tricky nipples pay my bills." Er, okay. That's a visual, thanks. Clearly, they had high thresholds for pain too, because whenever I asked questions like "Can you get an epidural before you go into labor?" they just smiled and showed me how to roll my hips back and forth on an exercise ball.

"This will help dilate your cervix as well as soothe the baby during the child-birth process."

Cool for the baby, but what about the mom-to-be, who clearly needed reassuring?

Infant CPR taught us to *never* under *any* circumstance leave our child alone with an uncut grape. Ten years later I still experience sweaty palms and tachycardia whenever I see a fruit bowl at one of his friends' houses. Who are these irresponsible heathens leaving full, intact suffocation blocks masked as healthy snacks on full display? *What if my child just helped himself to a piece of fruit and no one was there to cut it into quarters? Shouldn't they be locking that up?* We eat ice cream at our house because *melting* foods lower the risk of choking. Oh, yes, my anxiety goes deep. We're talking the Nine Hells deep. These "prep" classes triggered new pits of despair like a rogue wearing clown shoes tripping a trapdoor.

Then Bart almost got us kicked out of car seat safety class (and our unborn baby rehomed). We were practicing how to properly buckle and unbuckle a doll into a five-point harness when one of the straps got jammed and he upended the car seat and attempted to *shake the doll baby free.* I can still hear Patty and Jo, the self-proclaimed car seat queens, yelling across the classroom.

"He's tipping over the baby! Please never tip a baby, sir!"

I almost passed out watching a video in our labor and delivery class. And of course, the breastfeeding techniques class left me more confused about my own anatomy than that time in third grade when my friend and I discovered her mother's copy of *Fear of Flying.* Did I even have those parts? Basically, Bart and I had a better chance of wrestling Tiamat into footed pajamas than getting this kid out my body, home from the hospital, and fed.

When we weren't attending birthing school, Bart and I tried quelling each other's fears with our own version of one-on-one D&D by running each other through terrifying encounters.

BART: He gets a stomach bug, and it's highly contagious! You are the only one who can comfort him. What do you do?

ME: Hire a nanny willing to undergo a *Face/Off*-esque surgery to play me every time vomit, loose teeth, or snot is involved.

ME: He sneaks into your office, takes all your G.I. Joes off the shelf, opens the packaging, and asks you to come play with all the cool new dolls he found.

BART: First, did he really call them dolls? Because he's grounded. Forever. And going to boarding school. They are *action figures.*

We truly felt like 1st level adventurers alone in a dungeon with a tarrasque. The fear was mostly on behalf of our unborn child. What fresh hell did he generate in a past life to return to this plane as our offspring? But there was nothing we could do except overprepare, overthink, and pile on the crippling apprehension. Every blog post read and nugget of unsolicited advice received was like being on the receiving end of an evil druid's *thorn whip* spell, hurling us further into the abyss.

"Think of it like Christmas," my more maternally gifted friend said. "It's all a surprise! You don't know what you're getting, just that you'll love it. Well, more than likely love it. I mean, you might not love it at first, but it grows on you."

Not quite, I thought. I knew exactly what I was getting for Christmas, thanks to my heavily curated and highly distributed Amazon wish list. Also, I don't love surprises—or rather, the anticipation of a surprise, which yes, I understand is the whole point of a surprise. I knew a baby would eventually exit my body, but when? And where? I was scarred by those stories of babies falling out of their amniotic sacs and into toilets, forcing shocked, unsuspecting women to fish them out by their umbilical cords! If it can happen to twenty-three-year-old Tammy in a Chili's bathroom, it can happen to anyone.

Okay, everybody just calm down! (Or just me? Cool. Got it.) It may feel as though you have been dropped straight into the harrowing and chilling mists of Ravenloft. What holy terror awaits beyond that fog and gloom? Oh look, there's feared and famed vampire and wizard Strahd von Zarovich, and he needs your help baby proofing Castle Ravenloft! (Start with a sturdy child gate blocking off that living, pulsating demon tower.) But you will eventually find a beacon in the darkness. In fact, the mere promise of a beacon was enough to keep me going in those very early postpartum days. "It gets better!" That's what everyone says. "Why would they keep procreating otherwise?" People enter parenthood every day as they have for hundreds of thousands of years, and they've done it with a lot less technology, support, and caftan-clad birth goddesses. Did our parents ever get advice? Because us Gen Xers were raised unrestrained and backward in station wagons and playpens patrolled by our six-year-old cousins while the adults drank gin and tonics and played pinochle in another room. And we're *fine*. Just look at us.

What we lacked in skills we made up for in tangible goods. We had lots of books, geriatric dogs, sugary snacks, and games. Before he was even a plus sign on a pregnancy test, Bart got our son his very own copy of *The Hobbit* and a first edition *Monster Manual*. I bought all new cake decorating supplies in anticipation of a new crop of birthday parties. Oftentimes our "What would you do" encounters ended with "That would be really fun in a D&D game. But in real life . . ."

That's when it hit us. We *did* know what to do. Bart and I were essentially this kid's Dungeon Masters. While we couldn't tell him exactly how his quest would unfold or even how it would begin (hopefully not in a Chili's restroom), everything we needed to know was within the pages of the *Dungeon Master's Guide*. The same advice one might offer to a new DM happened to be great advice for new parents.

Have a Session Zero

A session zero is a chance for the players and Dungeon Master to talk about the upcoming campaign, manage expectations, make sure everyone is on the same page about the general themes and tone, and establish boundaries. Session zeros are key to starting off on the right foot. They also help the party bond.

The same concept can be applied by new parents. Find some time, ideally before that baby arrives, to have candid conversations with your partner, friends, and family about your parenting goals. What are you anxious about? What are you most excited about? Will you ignore a meltdown at a shopping center or carry your screaming child out surfboard style? How old should your child be before you let them eat a hot dog without being under your watchful eye? (The answer is eighteen. And make sure it's cut into tiny pieces.) Do you have a parenting style? (If you don't, that's okay. Dungeon Masters can help you discover that too!) This is not to say your "Only breastmilk for the first year" or "Only fifteen minutes of screen time a week" ideals won't change within the first thirty seconds of parenthood (and if they do, that is also totally fine), but practicing a swaddle on a watermelon is a great bonding exercise.

Prepare to Be Unprepared

There are a few things most Dungeon Masters do in advance of running a game. They read at least part of the adventure, take a few notes, gather up some minis and terrain if they use accessories, and show up. But even if you read an adventure from cover to cover, there's no guarantee that's how it will play out, and really, who wants it to? Once that book's spine is cracked and the party is gathered, that story becomes *yours*.

Players don't know any of the things DMs prepare, and that's how it should be. When we pull up a seat at the table, we are agreeing to a level of trust and open-mindedness. There will be twists, traps, tangential plot points, undiscovered locations, and unreliable narrators. The same is true when expecting a bundle of joy. Almost every parenting book aims to prepare parents for the next eighteen years, but it's much more practical to live in willful ignorance. You don't know what kind of baby you're getting, so how can you prepare? (Even my mom's psychic didn't know, so that was a waste.) Bart and I spent hours prophesizing. Would he be a good sleeper? (Oh, please!) Would he be chill and laid back? (Like his dad.) Or gassy and irritable? (Like his mom.) It's a roll of the dice. Just wait and see. All we could do was hope some kind of parental instinct would kick in and accept that it was okay to not have all the answers.

Fall in Love with Surprises

There's this gray area between "being unprepared" and "open to surprises," and it's heavily populated with new parents frantically running around asking each other for advice. Imagine your D&D character waking up every day in the midst of a challenging encounter. You don't even know what level it is, only that you're woefully underequipped. But you keep trying, dodging a death-ray here, seeking cover from the claw of a twig blight there, trying to outwit or outlast the beast, and gaining experience and new tools for your arsenal. You do your best, knowing someday this small human will make important decisions about your late-in-life care. It's a constantly changing landscape fueled by many obstacles and a few rewards. *At first!*

The surprises around every turn are what we love about D&D. I don't want to know what's in the dungeon. I want our fighter to kick down the door, our rogue to determine if there are any traps, and our wizard to detect magic. I play characters who make irrational and impetuous decisions just to see what happens. Not all surprises are meant to keep you on your toes. Sometimes surprises aim straight for your heart in the form of hearing your baby laugh the first time or your toddler squealing with glee when you walk into a room or your tween asking if you want to watch a movie with them. Human parents don't have a spellbook, but we do have an adventurer's spirit, and adventure begins when you are willing to run into the arms of the unexpected.

I Don't Know, What Would *You* Do?

There was a *Far Side* comic many years ago with a dog attempting to lure a cat into a clothes dryer by taping signs on the walls that said "Cat Fud" with arrows leading straight into the dryer. The dog was hiding between the washer and the wall with a thought bubble over his head begging, *Oh please, oh please* . . . I do not condone animal-on-animal trickery, but there's something so earnest and relatable about that old dog praying the cat falls into his trap. He was for sure a Dungeon Master.

I have also felt like that curious kitty tentatively following breadcrumbs in hopes they'll lead to the ancient relic my party is searching for and getting caught off guard every time we walk right into the den of javelin-wielding goblins. Should have seen it coming, and yet. . . .

"What do you want to do?" may be the most asked question in Dungeon Master history.

"I don't know!" I want to shout. "What would *you* do? You read ahead!"

My coworker Chris is one of my favorite Dungeon Masters and a dad to four. He would never tell us players what to do—that's not his job—but we always fall into his literal and figurative traps the same as if he had made up signs with arrows and taped them to the wall. He's *that* good. And when we know we're about to do something colossally dumb, he furiously rubs his palms together and his thunderous laugh reverberates throughout every floor of the office. Literally *every single time*. The signs are right there in front of us and there we go. Right into the green devil's maw.

Chris admitted he's employed some DM tactics with his brood.

"With kids, you can't tell them what to do, because they'll 100 percent rebel against that," he said. "So, you have to make it seem like it's their choice."

And all this time I thought I was riddled with common sense and good judgment.

He continued, "I just try to guide them down a path of seemingly innocuous questions until they get to the answer themselves. They feel all smart and clever for doing so."

Yep. That's *so* Dungeon Master.

Autonomy is inspiring. Kids gain confidence, and parents don't come across as the overbearing yet well-meaning ogres that they truly are. *Perceived* autonomy is even better because you *get* to be that overbearing yet well-meaning ogre behind the scenes. Roleplaying through different scenarios also helps build those ever-important soft skills that are harder to teach, like empathy and critical thinking. All of Chris's kids have turned out great, so he must be onto something. And all his kids still play D&D with him, which speaks to his skills as a Dungeon Master.

Make Failure Fun

I was maybe the worst waitress in the history of waitresses. (Did my theater degree prepare me for nothing?) I forgot orders, couldn't carry more than two plates at a time, and said "Sure, we have that" about salad dressings we definitely didn't have, and then rather than ask my customers to choose something else, I snuck off to the 7-Eleven next door to buy a bottle of Hidden Valley Bacon Ranch with my tip money. And yet, the customers loved me. They actually requested to sit in my section. Maybe they knew they could ask for a Domino's pizza and I'd run down the street to get that too, or maybe being served by me was kind of like a weird form of reality TV mixed with dinner theater where you got to watch a sort of charming oaf try to make her rent money by forgetting to refill your bread basket. What I lacked in functional job skills I made up for with charisma. Bumbling can be endearing.

Completely sucking the air out of a room because you are inept and choking, on the other hand, is not so endearing, which is exactly what I did during an early DM attempt. I invited five of my nicest coworkers to spend their lunch watching me make a fool of myself. Even I was surprised by how bad I was, and my expectations were very low. I did not embrace failure—never even saw it coming—so when it came ambling toward me with arms outstretched, I shrieked and shoved it into the bushes. As the game skidded sideways, my panic was contagious. The group was visibly uncomfortable with how much I was *not* enjoying my turn behind the screen, which made me feel guilty and uncomfortable because I was ruining not just their good time but also their lunchtime until it became a vicious circle of guilt, awkwardness, and shame for forty-three excruciating minutes. Laugh, and the world laughs with you. Lose your sense of humor and the ability to ask for help, and your D&D party will drop rocks on their own heads to end their misery. It took more than a decade before I tried DMing again.

Many much more even-keeled Dungeon Masters taught me that failure should not be feared because that's where the best stories come from. Actor, writer, and

D&D fan Todd Stashwick said, "There are no bad dice rolls. Only good stories," and please excuse me while I figure out how to open a Todd Stashwick Etsy fan shop so I can plaster that little ditty across coffee mugs and dice bags.

It's the same with parenthood. About 99 percent of the time you won't have a clue what to do, and you will be the star of some big, juicy critical failures. But you know what? Your baby won't remember it. And even if they do, they probably won't know any better. *You* are all they know! It will be years before their brains are developed enough to start comparing you to their friends' parents.

Respect the Game, and the Game Will Respect You

Have you ever seen those roundups of parents sharing pictures of their kid mid-meltdown and the seemingly innocuous reason that set them off? They couldn't eat the skin of a banana, they couldn't pick up a toy they were sitting on, they couldn't pet the dog on the TV. Pretty sad, really. Those are legit reasons. Sometimes kids act out because they're tired or hungry or not feeling well, and true, sometimes it's indicative of a larger concern. But it's important to remember that *they're kids*. Toddlers gotta toddle.

Once, my son and I were enjoying a lovely breakfast when out of nowhere he was in the throes of the world's most epic meltdown. He wanted toast, and I gave him "warm bread." Of course, I wanted to shout "OMG, what do you think toast is?! You want to hear about *real* problems?!" But then I remembered he had only been in existence for three years and was still learning how to process the world. To someone with little control over his life (and no fully developed brain), warm bread might be disappointing if you're handing out Michelin stars to perfectly cut and crisp slices of bread. Besides, his real issue probably had nothing to do with what he was served for breakfast. (But eight years of training later, and I can honestly say that my toast-making skills are on point.)

Dungeon Masters are adept at keying in on the wants and needs of their players and figuring out ways to incorporate them into the game. Someone might long for an attuned gnome statuette that serves no practical purpose, and someone else might still be trying to earn the praise of their sister, who wants nothing to do with them. It might seem insignificant to others around the table, but if it's on their character sheet, it's probably important to them. The player might not even know the significance of it, but they always appreciate a DM who pays attention. There's no shame in that. (Or maybe there is. Who knows what Dungeon Masters say about us in their secret subreddits.)

Never Split the Party

Well, you made it this far without one of my beloved Real Housewives references, but I'm afraid that ends here. *Real Housewives of New Jersey* iconic cast member Teresa Giudice once said, "Family isn't always blood. It's the people in your life who want you in theirs; the ones who accept you for who you are." She also once said she was being "raw as a cucumber" and called someone "Heckyll and Jive," so, you know . . . grain of salt. Teresa isn't always on the right side of history, but she probably would make a pretty good cleric.

I mean, you could play D&D by yourself, but it's more fun with a group. Like the game, parenting benefits from collaboration and finding a group of people you would also want in your life who want you in theirs.

It may not *feel* like a party all the time (especially when most of the members are unshowered, overtired, unfed, and bruised from disassembling a Pack 'n Play), but the first rule of parenting partying is "no judgment." The second rule is "go home by 7:00 p.m."

Fake It till You Make It

The scent of weakness is stronger than whatever is emanating from a baby otyugh's diaper. (Aw, cute!) Babies are like dogs, and not just because they drool a lot and like rolling in mud. Despite 99 percent of their actions, kids don't want to be in charge. *Allegedly* they test boundaries because they want to make sure they exist. Boundaries give kids a sense of security. If you're the alpha (and, get this—you *are*!), be the one in charge. Or at least act like you are in charge. It's all about roleplaying, remember? Don't feel confident? Write yourself an inspiring backstory. Lack assurance in your skills? Stat up an overpowered, severely busted character. That's you! Not sure what the consequences of your tactics will be? Plot it out like a story hook. Give yourself advantage on all dice rolls. Forever. You are the world's greatest Dungeon Master, and don't let anyone tell you otherwise.

If all goes well, the player shall surpass the Dungeon Master, and the tables will figuratively turn one day. Your leveled-up adventurer might become your Dungeon Master, so you should probably give them that gnome statuette after all.

The Thirteen Traits of Highly Effective Dungeon Masters (and Parents)

What makes a great Dungeon Master? Let us list the ways. A great Dungeon Master is:

- Creative
- Compassionate
- Generous
- Good at voices
- Collaborative
- A great host
- In possession of cool dice and accessories
- Open-minded
- Quick thinking
- Accepting of feedback
- Empathetic

The catalog of attributes could pave the way from Neverwinter Wood to the Frozen Forest. Seems like the part list for an unattainable superhuman, but I have to believe that if Dungeon Masters didn't innately possess most of those admirable traits, they wouldn't be drawn to the job. The same traits that make Dungeon Masters great are exactly the same ones new parents will want to hone. You could read a bunch of advice books or watch a bunch of videos or trudge through sanctimonious, amateur, hyper-opinionated social media comments in groups supposedly conceived to support all parents without judgment, but where's the fun in that? (Okay, some of those comments are pretty entertaining. *Simmer down, Brenda! It's just cradle cap.*)

I'll spare you any further interactions with Brenda, unless Brenda also happens to be a Dungeon Master in addition to an expert on the overactive hair follicles of newborns, because today's lesson is how to become one of these all-knowing, hyper-enlightened beings known as Dungeon Masters.

A good Dungeon Master (and therefore, parent) is someone who:

- **Doesn't try too hard.** Ina Garten, otherwise known as the Barefoot Contessa, is a cookbook author, TV personality, and gourmet food purveyor. She's cultivated an entire empire teaching people how to become the consummate host without all the fuss. Why spend all your time basting lamb chops in the kitchen while your guests are sipping Aperol spritzes on the patio? You can *buy* a delicious pasta salad or chutney and serve it up in a beautiful dish, making it look homemade. Do that. The barefoot bare minimum.

  I've had some of the best games of my life with DMs who didn't prep until fifteen minutes before we took our seats. How is that even possible? Their philosophy? Just think about the basics. There's no point in fleshing out scenarios the party may never encounter. For parents, there are definitely a few base skills you should brush up on before bringing home baby: how to change a diaper, infant CPR, don't tip the baby out of the car seat. Also, rice cereal is considered a solid food and yet not solid at all. No wonder we are all confused.

- **Recognizes simplicity is best.** Ina would also agree that the simple choice is often the best choice. And when there are too many choices, it can get overwhelming for new players as well as new humans. We once introduced a friend to D&D who was so eager to play until faced with her first question: "What do you want to do?"

  "What can I do?" she asked.

  "Anything," we answered.

  "But . . . like what?"

  "Literally anything!"

  We could have done that all night but quickly realized she would probably have more fun *playing* D&D than asking questions about it. The DM narrowed it down for her.

  "Well, you could move somewhere safer or cast a spell from your list or use a weapon."

  What you think of as a simple task, like choosing a weapon or picking out an outfit for school or answering a question about what you feel like doing, can be a very real anxiety trigger. A curated list of options gives the illusion of choice and hints at more things to come.

- **Caters to all parties.** Unless you've played D&D with the same people your whole life, you may have noticed everyone does it differently. There are lots of play styles and personalities—just one of the things to love about this game. You may have also noticed that every kid is wildly different. One friend's kid (Baby A) was soothed by staring at ceiling fans. Another friend's kid (Baby B) bristled with outrage at the mere hint of air blowing across his face. Wouldn't you be so angry if you took the advice of Baby A's parents and spent a bunch of time and money outfitting your house with ceiling fans only to discover you had a Baby B? (Baby B is very cute and has a lot to offer. Circulating air just ain't his jam.)

- **Is skilled at improv.** A well-thought-out plan to a toddler is like a tower of wooden blocks laboriously built by some other poor sap. It's just begging to be destroyed. The savviest Dungeon Masters know players have the ability to, and likely will, flip the script at a moment's notice. Do you *really* think they'll accept the quest to weed out the doppelgangers in Waterdeep? Not when there's an unmanned ship docked at the harbor just itching to be commandeered!

The first rule of parenting is accepting that sometimes kids (I'm looking at you, toddlers) can be jerks. The second rule is understanding that they can't help it. The third rule is that they're also pretty awesome a lot of the time. And the fourth and most important rule is that if you wish to present an air of authority, you must also recognize you have no ability to back it up. I mean, you can try, but it's the ultimate exercise in futility. It's liberating, really, but also incredibly alarming. A great solution is to "Yes, and . . ." your way through your child's formative years. For those who don't have a *thee-a-turr* degree like me (or haven't read every *Saturday Night Live* cast member's memoir) "Yes, and . . ." refers to an iconic improvisational tactic where improvisers go all in on each other's ideas and build off of them. It's not just a recipe for some very funny performances; it also fosters relationships built on commitment and trust. "Yes, and . . ." doesn't imply you should never say no to your child. That's bananas. It's teaching you how to think on your feet and roll with whatever your child throws at you (like those blocks that were just toppled by another kid).

- **Is a good listener.** A parent's ability to listen while also tuning out is a lifesaver. Think of it as mental multitasking—it's literally the only way I can survive nineteen *Fortnite* battle recaps every day. Sure, everything your kid says is fascinating, just like everything your D&D hero does is mind-blowingly cool. The best DMs make you feel like you're the only heroes in the realms. They get you. They know what motivates you. They literally know where all the bodies you buried are and which ones will make you shriek with glee when they rise again. Dungeon Masters can wade through the seven different conversations happening in the game and IRL and still be able to key into the most crucial bit of information and surprise you with a super innocuous nugget from your backstory three sessions later.

You think I want to debate the efficiency of a Hunter bolt-action sniper rifle versus a grenade launcher? No, I do not. Do I know the difference between a Talonflame and a Teddiursa? No, I do not. Do I know what Lexi said to Lucas that he repeated to Ben who told Mia, which made Bella no longer like Theo? Of course I do, because I love playground gossip! Kids are relentless storytellers and will follow you from room to room like a revenant Roomba if you try to get away. It's a great way to meet your daily step goal. I love that my kid wants to tell me *anything*. Today it's basketball stats. Tomorrow it could be his first crush, or questioning the existence of birds, or speculation on which *Love Is Blind* couple will stay together, and in a few decades it could be "Come on, Mom, why is your hologram always in my way? Just give me the keys to the hovercraft!"

- **Is aware of limitations.** There's nothing wrong with challenging your players. It's how they level up! Same goes for kids. D&D offers great problem-solving, creative-thinking, and analytical skills practice, but Dungeon Masters know the difference between a *challenge* and an unwinnable situation. You don't want to set your kids up for failure, but letting them flounder a bit will set them up for future success. It's hard to not jump in there and save the day (especially when they're learning to tie their shoes and it's like *OMG, kid, we're thirty-five minutes late. Just throw on a pair of slippers!*), but do you really want your kid to be Velcro-dependent their entire adult life?
- **Is not afraid to break the rules.** Remember my mom's advice about choosing your battles? I return to it often, but not like a Dungeon Master. They are literally choosing their battles because they're the ones coming up with all the in-game encounters. For a game that comes with more than a thousand pages of rules, we all agree the most important one is: Do what's right for your party. Even if it means not following *any* of

the rules. (The people who get paid to make up those rules will back me up on this.)

There are a bunch of socially contrived norms parents feel pressured to fit into. Who cares if your kid wants to wear full Pikachu garb to their sibling's baseball game? Waffles for dinner? *Again?* Well, aren't you a fun parent! So, you let your kid watch twelve extra minutes of screen time on a Friday or *Poltergeist*[1] before their sixth birthday. Big whoop. The night terrors will subside by the time they graduate from college. Your one rule? Do what's right for your family. Oh, and *you* rule too.

• **Is willing to give agency.** Parents get so used to doing everything for those helpless infants that we sometimes forget to actually teach them the skills to become independent. One day I left my son's clothes on his bed before school as usual, but on this day he was utterly appalled by the shirt I picked out. Wow, when did third graders get so snobby about tiny triceratops on tricycles?

"I guess *you* could pick out your outfit," I said, surprised by how much I apparently enjoyed this ritual. Before I could even get to the aggressive part of my passive-aggressive statement, he was already pulling on basketball shorts (it was November in Seattle) and a Golden State T-shirt from the dirty clothes hamper. The hairs on the back of my neck bristled watching this egregious crime against fashion taking place before my eyes. Royal blue, gold, and red? Was that a marker stain on the collar? He'll freeze! He'll be uncomfortable! He'll get made fun of because his clothes are visibly dirty and smell like root beer! He'll be ruined forever! (Some kid *allegedly* walked around with a poop stain on the back of his pants in my third-grade class. Several years ago that same kid sold his start-up for a gazillion dollars. Everyone still talks about the alleged poop stain.)

But you know what? Who cares? We had six minutes to get fed and leave the house. In third grade, the first full year back in person after COVID-19, these kids had bigger things to focus on than a sassafras-scented clashing wardrobe.

---

1. Bart insisted I mention that this actually *is* a big deal and by no means should be allowed. He watched *Poltergeist* when he was eight and still can't look under a bed or sleep in a room too close to a tree.

"At least wear a sweatshirt," I said, handing him an adorable little hoodie dotted with sentient tractors. (I really should have updated his wardrobe.)

The best Dungeon Masters don't railroad or tell their players what to do. Even if there's an integral plot hook in town or a super intricate trap they spent weeks detailing in the cellar beneath the tavern, there are gentle ways to nudge the party to the left or right while still making them feel like they're in control. There's that autonomy again. For kids, start with small things like choosing what to make for dinner or what gift to get your favorite author. (She'd like an adult-sized tiny triceratops T-shirt, please.)

- **Is kind and empathetic.** You can't walk a mile in a toddler's shoes because they're very tiny. But can you imagine what it's like to have been a human for only 842 days and still trying to master symbolic thought? One of the greatest side effects of playing D&D is empathy. By experiencing life from a different point of view and interacting in worlds and with characters who are different from you, players develop empathy. Kids won't have the same problems your grown-up self has because they don't have jobs or bills to pay or aging parents (well, my kid has two of those). But they still have problems.

  Being a Dungeon Master requires empathy. It's your story, but it's the players' journey. You're there to help them grow and level up and have a good time, and to do so you must understand what motivates them. What's important? What are they afraid of? What can you do to make them succeed? Even if it makes little sense to you (toast versus warm bread), it's the ultimate exercise in altruism.

- **Is able to keep their sense of humor.** Did I ever tell you about the time my sweet infant had explosive diarrhea while strapped to me in one of those fancy cloth baby carriers? Sorry, TMI? (Just wait.) It's funny now—a decade later. (Actually, it was funny then too, for the eighty-five partygoers who witnessed my newborn's digestive-inspired interpretation of the prom scene from *Carrie*.) What's that old saying? If you don't laugh, you'll have to leave the party early because you're covered in poop? That's parenthood in a nutshell. There will be crappy (yes, pun intended), stressful, scary moments.

  You know what I love best about D&D? The inside jokes and "you had to be there" moments. How annoying were my coworkers and I after a lunchtime game, howling like a pack of shriekers about when Mooth, the cleric, maced an ooze, causing it to split in half, and the wizard asked if we could try canning it and casting *botulism* as a weapon and . . . oh yeah, you had to be there. This is how we bond, in and out of the game. The same will be true for the party you've formed to care for your little hero. The other day our son told Bart and me that we sure laugh a lot for two people who aren't that funny. No truer words, kid. And we have him to thank.

- **Is flexible.** Dungeon Masters have had their fair share of absentee or distracted players or games where the group just wants to kill everything, including the innocent NPC who gave the party directions to the nearest inn. Even though they had an entire series of puzzles and skill challenges worked out for the session, they don't just throw their minis in the air and say, "You jerks ruined everything! I'm going home," like they're some kind of inflexible, overly sensitive, middle-aged mom! They go with it. Why? Because they're the Dungeon Master and are evolved enough to know if the players had fun, that's all that matters. Plus, you're way more mature than a middle-aged mom.

  Parents could use a big reminder about this kind of altruism when things they meticulously prepared get blown up faster than a myconid sprout caught in a fireball. You will be late for everything. You will cancel anticipated plans at the last minute. You will watch someone else find and finish off your secret stash of salt and vinegar potato chips— the expensive ones that never go on sale. You'll have to leave a restaurant before your dessert arrives. Your sleep will be interrupted. You will worry uncontrollably about things you were once blissfully unaware of, like secondary drowning and hidden hair syndrome. (No need to google, let's move on.) Be free of the conventional and embrace your new arbitrary life. You're easy-breezy like Drew Barrymore in *50 First Dates*, who can't remember yesterday and so starts each day fresh and eager. What will this day bring? Probably germs and much snack-making and trying to pee with a small person on your lap.

- **Is a generous collaborator.** Parents, like Dungeon Masters, are the ultimate arbitrators of the rules, but that doesn't—and shouldn't—mean they're unable to take feedback from the players. It's everyone's story at the end of the day. As your kids get older, involve them in discussions on house rules. Ask them what they think are reasonable chores and fair compensation. (And then have a good laugh when your six-year-old thinks emptying a plate into a compost bin should net a three-figure allowance.) Have them find the perfect spot for a new houseplant. Let them make decisions on where to get takeout or what the family should do on Saturday afternoon (stay home and play D&D, obviously). A sense of purpose instills confidence and fosters a sense of belonging. Plus, little kids are oddly excited about brooms and dustpans, so take advantage while you can.

- **Is patient and understanding.** If there's anything the pandemic has taught us, it's that plagues happen and will throw your entire world into the Underdark. Schools close, childcare is gone, laundry rooms turn into offices, and essential workers are forced to the front lines. Loved ones are lost. Lots of people will wake up every day not knowing if their jobs are secure or if businesses will survive. Learning how to reduce a fraction again isn't great, either. Many of us never felt so scared and helpless.

I know lots of Dungeon Masters who feel like they're not doing a good enough job, which is bonkers! Just *doing* the job is more than enough! Parents feel the same. Patience isn't just for watching your three-year-old eat spaghetti. You, the parent, deserve it too. Despite what books and sit-coms and your favorite parenting blogs make you think, this stuff is *hard*. But you don't need to be a fantasy hero to disable a trap or cure a wound. You don't have to memorize a spellbook to detect evil and good. You already are an innate spellcaster, a fighter of foes, and a bearer of constant inspiration, and you possess the most powerful spell in the universe: *your intuition*. You are someone's parent. If you're questioning how well you're doing the job, you're already crushing it.

Top Twenty Things Both Dungeon Masters and Parents Say

1. Are you sure you want to do that?
2. Put down your device and listen to me!
3. Oh really? I could ask you to do a lot worse.
4. We can do this one of two ways.
5. This is not a negotiation.
6. I cooked, I cleaned, I planned all of this for you! The least you could do is be grateful!
7. Just because you can, it doesn't mean you should.
8. Let me think about it.
9. Please just make a decision.
10. You did what?
11. Do you really think you should touch that?
12. What happened? It looks like a barbarian rage party in here!
13. How about you rest up first?
14. You're not going out dressed like that, are you?
15. This hurts me more than it hurts you.
16. Be careful.
17. I need a break. Can someone else take over?
18. Now what are you going to do?
19. It really shouldn't be this hard.
20. This would be so much easier if we just worked together.

To Market, to Market We Go!

Content Warning: This chapter briefly mentions sudden infant death syndrome (SIDS) as part of "The Calming Cleric Package" section, so please feel free to skip that part if needed for your comfort.

So, there I was, eight months pregnant, alone at Babies "R" Us. It was a Friday evening, and I was relishing how cool my soon-to-be-new-mom life was. I mean, it was a *Friday*, I was *very pregnant*, and I was at a mass-market baby store on the brink of bankruptcy. #bestlife

Now, you're probably thinking, *Wait, does she seriously think that's cool? Because this book is going right in the bin.* No, sweet child. I haven't been cool since that one day in 1987 when my best friend, Cindy, and I went to see *Coming to America* with the glorious hair band Cinderella. They even asked if we wanted to hang out after, but I had a math test the next day, so I had to go home.

You may also be thinking, *Babies, blah blah blah, can we please hear more about the teenage musical exploits of you and your friend Cindy?* Yes, you can! But that's going in a different book. This is a story about cotton balls. A cautionary tale, if you will.

Right, now you're thinking, *Why would you buy cotton balls at Babies "R" Us when every grocery store and drugstore sells them? Do babies require a special kind of cotton only found nestled between fake mustache pacifiers or designer poop bags? Also, what the heck is Babies "R" Us?* To that all I can say is "Wow. Can you just stop thinking so much and just enjoy the story?" Also I think it's sad if you truly don't know who Geoffrey the Giraffe is. He's only one of the greatest retail shills, right up there with the adorable teddy bear with sociopathic eyes that always has someone's laundry on his head. Geoffrey was so synonymous with kids and toys, he convinced me that not only do babies need cotton balls, but they must be purchased from a store that sells goods specifically for babies. My baby would know if I swabbed his body with cotton procured from a Safeway. I bought fourteen bags of cotton balls that day.

Turns out babies don't need that much cotton. Who knew? What did I think I would be doing with it? Spinning those fibers into threads to make his own clothes? Transforming his bedroom ceiling into a topography of marine strato-cumulus clouds representative of the Pacific Northwest? Maybe I could add pinecone snowy owlbear planters to my soon-to-be Etsy shop.

Here's something you need to understand about me: I live in fear of being unprepared, which I know is odd considering how many times I've told you it's totally fine to be unprepared. Just know that every time I write that: (A) it's my exposure therapy; (B) it's true; and (C) do as I say and not as the six outfit changes, toiletry bag, and box of emergency ration bars in the trunk of my car do. The "Top 200 Items You Need to Prepare for a Newborn" lists are writ-ten for pregnancy preppers like me. They capitalize on our insecurities. They give us a false sense of confidence by making us believe that if our homes are stocked with enough cotton to stuff a life-size plush Geoffrey monument, our children will be born sleep trained and bypass all the daycare waitlists. They lure us into mass-market specialty stores to purchase items in excess we probably already have in our medicine cabinets. (I did.) Even with my need to have the right equipment, I sometimes overlook the basics. This is true of the fantasy me as well.

Once my D&D character left a well-stocked town in search of adventure with just the robes on her back.

"How much rope do you have?" the Dungeon Master asked the party when we were about to scale a cliffside.

"Plenty," I answered confidently.

"Do you have a light source?" the Dungeon Master asked the party when we approached the dark mouth of the cave.

"Got a lamp!" I said, sure that had to be part of the whole starting equipment package.

"And oil?" the Dungeon Master asked.

"Oil, check. Sure do!"

"Let me see your character sheet," he said, spinning my laptop to face him.

Turns out I didn't have any light source, let alone oil, my fifty feet of rope was wrapped around the limb of a grandfather tree back in the High Forest, and I donated most of my rations to the retired familiars' convalescence home I invented and had made the party volunteer at for an afternoon. I did have a piece of leather, some arrows (although no bow), and an abacus I won from a dwarf in a card game. So, you know, the fantasy equivalent of a pallet of cotton balls. I thought starting equipment, like our coinage, was *assumed* or not actually audited by the Dungeon Master. Do people even fill out that section of their character sheet?

The whole concept of inviting a baby into your home is rife with consumerism. From the very moment you even think about pregnancy, your wallet opens and dollars fly out of it, and suddenly your bathroom is filled with prenatal vitamins, ovulation kits, multiple pregnancy tests (because it takes at least six to ensure a positive is *really* positive), a basal body thermometer, and 437 books explaining fertility, the female reproductive system, and how hard it actually is to get pregnant. Seriously. There's like a two-and-a-half-minute window every month where our bodies will even entertain the idea.

Outfitting a new D&D character might feel a whole lot like preparing for the first baby. Your newest hero wants to make a good first impression, and you want them to have the right gear. (You also want a big mug of mead and a long rest in a quiet inn, but let's get you some cotton balls first.) This one is going to fall largely on parents, because even though your baby registry might include important equipment like sleep monitors and car seats, your loved ones will load you up on baby bathrobes and socks with tiny rattles attached to their toes.

It's a daunting quest, but if you approach it how your character (yours, not mine) prepares for their next big gig, it's less overwhelming.

Gather your gold and get shopping for the most practical tools needed in anticipation of your biggest adventure yet.

Starting Equipment

There are a few things every newborn adventurer should have regardless of their class.

- **Diaper bag:** Consider this your *bag of holding*. It will go everywhere your baby goes and for the first ten months will house more gear than an REI warehouse sale. Backpack styles are great because they'll leave your hands free for carrying other things, like a baby.
- **Diapers:** I mean, I *think* this one is pretty obvious? You can likely find a subscription service that delivers them straight to your door, because it's shocking how many times you come close to running out.

- **Car seat:** The hospital won't let you leave without one, and if they told me that before I gave birth, I might not have brought ours. *KIDDING.* But if you plan on ever transporting your child in a vehicle, you're going to need a car seat and a 17th level wizard to not only help you research all of the different makes but also install it. What you won't need is a good pair of beefy forearms, because after two weeks of lugging that thing around, you'll be all set.

The Practical Protector Package

Keeping the baby safe and surveilled is your number one priority.

- **Crib:** Did you know babies sleep a lot? Unless they're a baby elf, in which case they'll just meditate a lot. Babies have no shame in their sleep game. They'll just drop into a slumber in the crook of an elbow, a jumper suspended from a door frame, even a bowl of mashed sweet potatoes. They're not picky, but as their primary caregiver, you should strive for a bit more structure. While your druid ranger might rough it on a bedroll, it's safe to say zero out of a million pediatricians would recommend letting your little slumber lover snooze unencumbered. *Note:* It's recommended you keep all soft bedding, including stuffed animals, out of the crib until your baby is twelve months old.
- **Baby monitor:** Can you cast *arcane eye*? Are you a dwarf with dark-vision? No? Then you're going to need a little help in the surveillance department. Baby monitors have grown up quite a bit from the one-way talk intercom devices they were when I was a kid. They pan, they zoom, they monitor the room temperature, and they play lullabies. A good monitor is a must as it offers parents a sense of security and a modicum of freedom to wander about the house, which of course instead they'll spend on the couch, enraptured by the view of their snoozing baby.
- **Changing table and changing pads:** I once heard a story about *some mother* who changed her baby on the heavily trafficked tile floor of a public restroom. Okay, it was *one time* and technically he was on my coat, so really it's me you should feel sorry for in this scenario.

    Assume you are at home and need to change your baby. (You should definitely assume this.) You might think, *Well, I'm at home! I can do that anywhere. It's not like I'm laying my vulnerable child down on a floor coated with the bodily fluids of strangers!* Okay, first, *stand down*, Brenda.

I said it was one time and he was on my coat, which I parted with shortly after this incident, so again I ask, *Who do we feel sorry for in this story?* Second, think carefully about where it's appropriate to change a diaper. Do you have any idea what you will find in a diaper? Do you want that on your dining room table or new bedspread? Because it will spread. On your bed. Sometimes it will spray or erupt like a geyser. You get what I'm saying? Third, a changing table is ergonomically correct, and it's so much easier to change a diaper without a pulled a trapezius. Plus you can have all those baby changing supplies you panic-bought right at your fingertips. They also make great napping spots for cats.

Don't forget to get portable changing pads to keep in your diaper bag and multiple covers for the pad at home. Changing pads need changing too.

The Calming Cleric Package

- **Pacifiers:** Perhaps you think, *Not my baby!* Pacifiers are more contentious than the debate over how much damage a character would take if they were thrown off a spelljammer. I'm pretty sure my kid left my body with a pacifier jammed into his tiny baby mouth, but despite Bart's worries, it appears he will not be going to college with one. I'm not sure who was more dependent on these things—him or us. Our son called his pacifier a "me-me" because he used to point at it and yell "Me! Me! Me!" Before long all the kids at his daycare were all screaming for their pacifiers by shouting "Me! Me! Me!" I'm super proud of the legacy my kid left behind.

  At night we used to drop a dozen or so me-mes into his crib, scattering them around like breadcrumbs so that if one fell out of his mouth, he'd be able to find another close by rather than wake up crying. We called it the me-me farm. The choice to use one is totally up to you, and there are lots of pros and cons on both sides. No judgment here!

  ✳ **Pro:** Pacifiers can be excellent distractions, and studies have shown they may reduce the risk of sudden infant death syndrome (SIDS).[1]

---

1. Sudden infant death syndrome, also is known as SIDS, is the unexplained death of a baby. But some research points to it being caused by problems in the area of an infant's brain that controls breathing and waking up from sleep. Your doctor will be able to provide more information.

* **Con:** You will spend the equivalent of a family of five's monthly grocery bills keeping these things stocked in your car, in the house, in the diaper bag. The fear of losing your baby's favorite one is real (and they always have a favorite; RIP blue me-me). Also, it's a hard habit to break. In order to get our son to stop using one, we crafted a whole story about a me-me fairy who would collect me-mes to give to the Feylost children from the Feywild in exchange for treasure. Fortunately, our kid was very treat motivated.

• **Sleep monitor:** Different from the baby monitor in that these devices can also measure vital signs, including pulse and blood oxygen saturation rate. An alarm will usually sound if the rates fall below preset levels. Nothing calms a new parent's nerves like waiting for a siren to go off!

• **First-aid kit:** Hopefully you never need to use it, but it's better to be stocked up in case a healing word won't cut it. Your first-aid kit for a baby should include a number of items from Band-Aids to baby pain medication to, yes, even cotton balls. Make sure all items are created for newborns! Other items you'll want to include are (but not limited to—check with your pediatrician):

* **Gas drops or gripe water:** Is it gas or a smile? Is it gas or colic? Is it gas or did someone cast *cloudkill* up in here? Most likely it's gas, so stock up!

* **Baby nail clippers:** Whoa, did someone give birth to a mezzoloth? Babies' fingernails might be their fastest-growing body part, and I'm here to say "Ouch!" Take 2d8 slashing damage every time their fingernails make contact with your skin.

* **Saline nose drops:** Babies can't blow their nose. As it turns out, some ten-year-olds can't blow their nose, so make sure to have this trusty booger de-gluer on hand. But wait—you think that's gross? Read on.

* **Nasal aspirator:** Remember those squishy, bulbous rubber syringe devices that resemble water towers? They're essentially vacuums that gently suction out mucus from a baby's nostril. You can go old-school analog or get an electric version. And that's not even the grossest one!

* **NoseFrida:** Aka the Snotsucker, this is by far the most disgusting thing you'll ever own, but I promise you'll be glad you have it. I have indeed done just what the product promises. Parenthood makes you do all sorts of weird things. Let's move on, shall we?

✴ **Butt cream:** And somehow cream for butts doesn't seem that gross anymore. Your baby's bum will thank you. Or maybe I was so sleep deprived I hallucinated that entire conversation.

Spellcaster Package

Magic comes in all forms in the real world. Use up all your spell slots to acquire these charming mechanisms.

- **Sound machine:** Sadly, Gloria Estefan is not included. Babies, like puppies, must be desensitized to everyday sounds like doorbells, sirens, lawnmowers, and *Sex and the City* reruns. The neighbor mowing their lawn doesn't care if your baby is napping. Your child will be invited to sleepovers or go to camp or live in a dorm. Having the TV on in the living room probably won't wake them. It will get them used to sleeping through common interruptions. But that's what the daytime is for. At night babies need to catch some uncompromised *Z*'s. Whether it's an app, a machine, or a stuffed sheep (like the Sleep Sheep), consider white noise the white knight of a good night.
- **Diaper Genie:** This genie only offers one wish, and that's "Make this foul pouch of poo be gone!" Hopefully when this genie perishes, it doesn't leave behind what it was carrying.
- **Sophie la Girafe:** Legend has it, around the age of nine months, Sophie la Girafe visits little French babies, and the next day their mouths are magically filled with perfect little baby teeth. (What is it with babies and giraffes anyway?) I have never attended a baby shower that this little François rubber chew toy didn't also attend. She's *the* teething toy, and now we know why so many American babies grow up to be Francophiles.

Armor One for All

Not all protective gear needs to be made of chain mail or metal.

- **Swaddle blankets:** The hardest thing I ever had to do for my child was figure out how to swaddle. There were not enough nurses or YouTube videos to properly wrap a relatively immobile seven-pound newborn into a tight—but not too tight—muslin cocoon. Swaddling soothes and calms babies, making them feel like they did in the womb, and really does seem to lull them to sleep. But figuring out all the tucks, wraps, and folds is a bit of an art form, so practice early, practice often.

- **Sleep sacks:** Eventually babies outgrow swaddling, and until they can safely sleep with a blanket, they need other means for staying warm and toasty while they snooze. Enter the beloved sleep sack, basically a soft, zippered, loose-fitting, lightweight sleeping bag with holes for the arms and head. You will never envy your child more than when you tuck them into this cozy little sleep treat.
- **Burp cloths:** This armor is for you because spit-up happens.
- **Wardrobe basics:** Babies love an outfit change! It's hard to look fashionable when diaper butts and teething rings are involved, and yet babies nail it every time. It's hard to resist tiny argyle vests and khakis with crotch snap closures, and really, why should you? In our son's case, he eventually won't want to wear anything but oversized pajama bottoms and Crocs, so enjoy the faux elbow-patched cardigans while you can.

There's so much to consider (and store) for your child, and it's easy to get overwhelmed. If your starting equipment arrives before your baby does, you'll be well equipped for your first adventure. Easy on the cotton balls, though.

Top Ten Misconceptions about
Dungeons & Dragons *and* Parenting

1. There are too many rules.
2. I don't have the time.
3. I will miss my discretionary income.
4. I do not possess the skills needed.
5. I'm not buying the fantasy.
6. None of my friends will do it with me.
7. Aren't you, like, committed to it forever?
8. I have to do silly voices all the time.
9. I'm not going to be good at it, and everyone will laugh at me.
10. I don't make deals with demons.

Let's Party!

Got a hot tip on how to cool off a colicky baby? What about the bead on swim lessons? Know anyone who can wrangle a dozen lop-eared bunnies for a birthday party? Maybe not, but your network of parents might.

It has been said that your D&D adventuring party will be the most meaningful relationship you will ever have. Where was that said? Right here. You literally just read it. And I believe it. Where else can you have epic, death-defying adventures born of stories crafted from your collective imagination? Those are bonding moments and they carry through in real life.

The first time I played D&D it was with coworkers who were relative strangers and I was also being forced to learn how to play this bizarre, mathy, weird dice-rolling fantasy *game* because it was relevant to my day job. What even was a roleplaying game? Was this like drama therapy? Would I *need* therapy after having spent two hours in a windowless conference room with an ad trafficker who used an affected accent to bargain with an innkeeper and a bad shot paralegal with a penchant for acid arrows? What happened during those two hours was nothing short of real magic. Not only did we discover that the ancient stereotypes we harbored about Dungeons & Dragons were grossly outdated, not to mention flat-out wrong, but more incredulously, we became friends. Like actual outside-of-work friends. We played together every Monday for the next two and half years. I planned the barbarian's baby shower. The rogue made my son a beautiful bespoke Star Wars–themed keepsake box for his first birthday. The cleric officiated our wedding.

Pulling your shipmate onboard a spelljammer or using your bonus action to offer a healing word or sharing your rations because apparently your DM is just way too involved in how much equipment you're packing and you forgot to fill out that part of your character sheet can't help but connect you in real life. It's the concept of "bleed" so prevalent in games like D&D. Bleed, or roleplay bleed, is when the feelings or actions that happen in game affect the players outside of the game and vice versa. Your character and another are best friends, bonded since they were both orphaned after a war destroyed most of their homeland. You and that player are quick to develop feelings of affection for each other in real life. Conversely, a beloved party member might suffer an untimely fate in game, and the surviving party members aren't the only ones who suffer the emotional blow. The players might find themselves feeling depressed or anxious outside of the game. Bleed goes both ways. The point is, D&D is much more meaningful (not to mention successful) with an adventuring party. The same is true for your parenting game.

Think of other parents as your personal concierges or, better yet, your adventuring party. If you fall asleep in their presence, they'll cover you with a blanket, empty your dishwasher, entertain your baby, and be genuinely thrilled you managed to get in a short rest. They don't care if you showered or are covered in unidentified stains. No judgment if that basket full of clean laundry is now doubling as a jungle gym. Party friends can support you in a myriad of ways only those who have been through it can. You need these people, which is not to say you should dump your child-free friends. I'm pretty sure they'll be cool not giving their opinion on your kid's weird butt rash.

Allow me to share an actual transcript from a text thread between a group of moms to illustrate my point:

> **MOM 1:** Are you guys going to Jonah's birthday party?
> **MOM 2:** When is it?
> **MOM 3:** Oh crap, yes, I forgot to RSVP.
> **MOM 4:** I don't think Landon was invited. Phew!
> **MOM 1:** Saturday, 2pm
> **MOM 2:** Shoot, Brady has baseball tryouts at 1. I don't think we'll make it in time.
> **MOM 4:** Oh, yeah, Landon was invited. Email went to spam.
> **MOM 1:** I can pick up Cassidy and take her to the party. We'll be coming back from karate, which is right by the baseball fields. Riverview, right?
> **MOM 3:** Has anyone ever heard of dysgraphia?
> **MOM 2:** That would be amazing! I can pick up from the party and bring Eli home.
> **MOM 4:** What's Jonah into?
> **MOM 1:** Is it like dyslexia?
> **MOM 4:** Landon never talks about him. No idea who he is.
> **MOM 2:** I think *Fortnite*. Maybe *Pokémon*?
> **MOM 3:** It's a writing disability. I think Lucy might have it.
> **MOM 1:** Actually, I need to pick up a prescription from the compound

pharmacy on Saturday before they close. Could you keep Eli for like another hour? Traffic sucks coming from North Seattle.

MOM 4: Going to Target. Want me to pick up any gifts for Jonah?

MOM 2: Oh no! What's going on with Lucy?

MOM 3: I need a gift bag, please! Big enough for a board game.

MOM 1: Get me one of those dumb prairie dresses from Target! I haven't shaved in weeks and I could use all the covering up I can get.

MOM 2: Eli can hang as long as you need him to!

MOM 3: Mom 1, LOLOLOLOLOLOL they're so fugly! Why????

MOM 1: I have so many gift bags. PLEASE! Take them all!

MOM 4: Oh cool, can I have a gift bag too? Medium.

MOM 2: Anyone have a good rec for a children's orthodontist? It's that time . . .

MOM 3: She's really struggling with writing. The handwriting! It's indecipherable.

MOM 4: COVID.

MOM 2: COVID.

MOM 1: COVID.

MOM 3: Yeah, I thought COVID, but we worked on it all through COVID. She's not behind in anything. Just has a really hard time with writing.

MOM 4: When do we stop blaming COVID?

MOM 2: #never

MOM 3: Oh, that reminds me, did you hear Tyler has COVID? He sits right next to Rowan, so I guess our three-year streak is up.

MOM 1: Dr. Wexler! My niece just got braces. She loved him!

MOM 4: Lucy's valentine to Landon looked fine. I mean, no worse than any other kids.

MOM 2: Tyler's had that cough for two years. Maybe it's not COVID.

MOM 3: I "helped" with those valentines. She was getting so frustrated I couldn't stand it.

MOM 1: I think Tyler has asthma. He does cross-country with Eli's friend. It's not . . . great.

MOM 3: So, I guess my handwriting is on par with a fourth grader who was homeschooled for two years? 😅😅😅😅😅

MOM 4: Happy hour Friday?

MOM 1: . . .

MOM 2: . . .

MOM 3: I found a gift bag!

MOM 1: I can do Friday from 5–5:35! Let's go!

MOM 2: Pete has a work thing, so I have the kids. Want to come over though? Pizza? Beer? Bring the kids?

MOM 4: Kids? I'm out. 😖

MOM 3: OMG I can keep my sweatpants on? Yes, please.

MOM 1: In. What can I bring?

MOM 2: Gift bags!

That's the thing about your parent friends. (And extra shout-out to all moms who are probably right now feeling guilty for reading a book and not ticking something off their to-do list.) They're always ready to pick up your slack and offer you a gift bag. Okay, I guess that's two things. And there's about a million more, which is why you need to start forming your parenting party even before you're expecting.

While your road to parenthood won't be the same as someone else's, there are fundamental commonalities parents can all relate to. Namely, it's hard. Like *really* hard. Even the most accomplished progenitor hits rough patches and feels like throwing in the ol' burp cloth. But it's also mind-blowingly awesome, and awkward, and funny, and uncomfortable, and a whole host of other adjectives that I add to the list daily, and let's be honest—pictures of your kid from tumbling class or imitating the cute way they say "amember" instead of "remember" aren't super entertaining if you don't have your own similar tales to tell. It's like when someone tells you about their dream. Am I in it? Did I do something cool? Because otherwise, it's probably not as interesting to me as you think it is. You can love being a parent and hate the frustration and angst that comes with it. You can love your children and still want nothing more than to get away from them. Emergency dental appointments and band concerts crop up, forcing you to cancel plans or take a long time to return a text. Your A game is . . . well, D– at best. Other parents get it. They probably don't even remember sending the text it's taken you six weeks to return. It takes a hamlet to raise a kid. Don't go at it alone.

But how do you make friends with other parents? It's hard to make any friends as an adult, let alone tired, overcommitted, emotionally unstable ones. There may have been a time when you thought D&D was hard to learn too, and look at you now, 18th level armorer artificer hexblade warlock! Still not convinced? Because you're likely a gamer, let's talk about this in familiar terms.

Before you plunk down your hard-earned cash on a new game, you probably read reviews, right? Well, let's hear what other parents are saying about their procreator posse.

Unconditionally nonjudgmental!
"Parents have been there, done that, and if they haven't, they're about to! We all go through it. Being judgy is a surefire way to ensure you're going to get bit in the butt. (Spending too much time in the two's room at daycare is another surefire way.) Anyone who lives in fear of bad karma will make a great ally!"

—Keely, mom to three under five

Parents offer free childcare to other parents!
"I had just a few essential items to get from the grocery store and was going to be gone no more than twenty minutes. My neighbor offered to watch Sam for me. I can't tell you how great it felt to not have to navigate the stupid pirate-ship shopping cart the size of a superyacht around seven hundred Pringles cans stacked in a precarious Christmas tree formation! As an added bonus, Sam entertained her kids so she could get some work done around the house. Highly recommend!"

—Jack, Sam's dad

Next-gen adventuring party in the works!
"Know who likes attending birthday parties for one-year-olds? Other one-year-olds. Know who doesn't? Everyone else. Sorry, not interested in spending my Saturday afternoon in someone's backyard watching little Riley shove an organic, sugar-free, gluten-free Bundt cake into their eye socket. Doesn't this kid have any friends under the age of thirty-five?"

—Marin, child-free coworker who does not
want an invitation to Riley's birthday party

Dad talks about his baby all the time while other dads listen!
"Don't ask a D&D player about their character if you don't have four hours to dedicate to their multi-classing manifesto detailing every hero they ever worshipped since discovering the game thirty-five years ago. Even other D&D players have their limits. You can, however, talk about how your kid is learning sign language or your baby's refusal to potty train in the company of other parents. Bring photos and expect reciprocation!"

—Sean, dad to Finnegan and Siobhan,
both of whom are potty trained

Parents exhibit casual, sometimes gross, behavior in front of each other and remain friends!

"I went to another mom's house on three different occasions and it was clean every time! What kind of dark magic are they practicing over there? I eventually stopped returning her calls. It's hard to get comfortable on a couch not covered in popcorn and gummy worms."

—Kari, mom of eleven-year-old twins

Hand-me-downs receive 100 metascore!

"It's fun buying clothes for a baby until they're about six months old. Then it's all function over fashion. There's barely any fabric here. I'm spending a monthly car payment on sparkle leggings! It's madness! Thankfully a family with kids a few years older moved in down the street. As soon as their kids outgrow something, it's all out with our old and in with their old."

—Aaron, a fed-up girl dad of three

You're right, Aaron. It *is* madness (but sparkle leggings are the bomb).

Mom accidentally tells child-free coworker how much daycare costs. HER RESPONSE WILL SHOCK YOU!

"I don't care how many times my coworker's new baby woke her up last night or what the difference is between magnet and charter schools. I do care if you bring hand, foot, and mouth disease into the office. Venting is a very normal, necessary part of parenting, I'm sure. Just know your audience, please."

—Janice, blissfully child-free coworker,
currently working remotely from the
Dominican Republic

Okay, ready to plunk down your hard-earned money on your parent party? Too bad because they're free. (Or at least they *should* be. I haven't figured out how to monetize cooing over other people's kids yet.) Similar to wanting to learn a new game, there are rules to learn, and you'll probably have a few questions. I got you.

FAQs: How to Make Friends When You're an Awkward Adult Who's Got a Bit of a Temporary Identity Crisis

Parent friends sound great, but where might one find these magical unicorns?

❋ Same way you might find your next gaming group. First, look around. Do you see anyone wearing something with a giant red ampersand on it? Start there. You might at least find your next Dungeon Master, and by now you should know what awesome people they are. Daycare or preschool is a prime spot to pick up parenting friends. Your kids will be spending all day together, so they're already familiar. And lots of schools have social events, Facebook groups, or group texts so you can get to know the other families from the safety of your keyboard before gaining the courage to meet up IRL. New-parent support groups are often formed based on neighborhood and due date, so you can likely find other families with kids the same age right in your neighborhood. Schools are an obvious choice too. If there's one thing parents want, it's for their kids to have friends. As soon as my son mentions another child's name, I've got mini corn dogs in the oven and IPAs in the cooler, ready to entertain the whole family.

How do I make the first move? I'm awkward, remember?

❋ My dog has more friends than I do. Every day on our walks we say hi to Baily, Viggo, Juno, Jax, and Simba. I have no idea what their humans are called or what color hair they have, and yet we make eye-contactless chit-chat for several minutes on the daily. Puppy is old and not really looking to hang, but if I were looking for a few canine companions, I could easily ask Jax's human if she'd like to go for a walk sometime or enjoy ripping the squeaker out of a stuffed skunk in our backyard.

❋ Asking out a parent friend is even less awkward. You're at the playground the same time every day, your kids are the same age, and they already play together. Time to take it to the next level and ask if the other parent would like to check out the science museum next time. Eventually you're sharing Cheddar Bunnies, then phone numbers, then Capri Sun mixers for your cocktails.

❋ Kids, like D&D, are nothing if not a great common denominator and icebreaker.

I literally just had a baby. I'm terrible company! Who would want to be my friend?

✽ I told you the old adage "misery loves company" was about parents, remember? Consider yourself "company," and all the new friends you're about to make are "misery." They're gonna love you! The thing about parent friends is that you don't *have* to be good company. They get it. No explanation necessary, and it's way less pressure for them. They've been there. Probably five minutes ago. Not every day is a critical hit, but you don't always have to be the hero. Sometimes you just get to assist. Just like on the days your dice are rolling 1s, your friends will pick up the slack.

Who is asking these questions? You're just talking to yourself, aren't you?

✽ Yes.

What do I do with my child-free friends? Am I supposed to ditch them? Are they going to ditch me?

✽ Oh no, no, no! It's not *their* fault you decided to procreate! While it's true you'll be less available and maybe not quite as good company in the early years as before, but you became friends for a reason. Yes, you're a parent. It's an important, often time-consuming gig. But it's not your sole identity. Even you will get tired of the baby talk. Spending time with people who have never strained a pea or contemplated the pros and cons of Reggio versus Montessori is refreshing.

Moppet Manual: Toddling Terrors

Beware the temperamental Toddling Terror! Young Toddling Terrors who have just gotten a taste of independence are nearly impossible to tame. They have never met a border they didn't test or a button they didn't press. Innately curious and impetuous, Toddling Terrors are prone to bad decisions and making noise, and any attempt to rein them in will be met with public displays of resistance.

They often delight in each other's company and are more dangerous in packs. The collective yowl of a tower of Terrors is enough to make a banshee run into the sunlight. However, Toddling Terrors have no loyalty and will turn on each other at the slightest provocation, perceived or imagined. Toddling Terrors lack all reasoning capabilities, but in some cases they can be charmed by moving pictures (especially those of cartoon dogs in first-responder gear or steam trains with weird faces) and incapacitated for long stretches of time. In melee they resort to biting their prey and immediately placing blame on another Terror.

Toddling Terrors like routine only so that they can kick it in the teeth. However, should they stray from their routine, they will become even more irrational and aggressive. Do not tell a Toddling Terror they are tired. *They are*, but they mustn't be told so. Their moods change more often than a Shrieking Enchanter's diaper. When threatened or—in the rarer case—captured, the bones of Toddling Terrors vanish, rendering them impossible to carry or hold on to. They get +16 to all attacks in areas where there are large crowds. Toddling Terrors feed off an audience. Sometimes literally.

They cannot put on their own shoes.

➤ **Best Defense:** *Food.* Toddling Terrors enjoy putting objects in their mouths and sometimes exhibit small bouts of mercy toward those who offer to feed them.

TODDLING TERROR
Small fey, Chaotic Evil

Armor Class 8
Hit Points varies, depending on the day
Speed 20 ft toddling; 160 ft toddling unattended in dense, dangerous, difficult environs

---

STR	DEX	CON	INT	WIS	CHA
4	0	1	2	1	22

Skills Acrobatics +4, Sleight of Hand +6, Investigation +4
Senses Tremorsight 40 ft, passive Perception 12
Languages Babble, Partial-Common, High-Pitched, Unprovoked Wailing
Condition Immunities exhaustion, grappling, incapacitated, prone, restrained, stunned
Challenge 18 (27,000 XP)

Circle Time. Anytime a creature other than a Toddling Terror is within 100 feet of one or more Toddling Terrors and is subjected to their screeching must make a DC 15 Wisdom saving throw. On a failure, the creature is stunned until the start of their next turn. On a success, the creature must enter the circle and perform a song and dance until the Toddling Terrors get bored, tired, or distracted by another creature, which can take anywhere from 30 seconds to 3 days.

Squishy. The Toddling Terror can move through spaces 6 inches wide. They are incredibly bendy and drawn to gates, cat doors, and cable zip ties usually in place to keep them safe.

Repetition of Song. The Toddling Terror can keep only one song in their brain at a time and must keep singing this song lest they forget it. Every humanoid within 300 feet of the Toddling Terror that can hear the song must succeed on a DC 20 Wisdom saving throw or be driven to madness by the current song until the Toddling Terror moves on to another song, in which case the humanoid must attempt another DC 20 Wisdom saving throw. On a failed saving throw, an actual earworm will burrow into the humanoid's ear, causing them to not just hear the Toddling Terror's song on an endless loop, but sometimes belt it out at inopportune moments such as during a job interview or undergoing a pelvic exam. In addition to burrowing the song into your brain, the earworm causes 1 point of psionic damage everyday it is not destroyed and replaced by another earworm.

ACTIONS
Bite. *Sneak Attack*: +10 to hit, reach 10 ft, 1 target. *Hit:* 22 piercing damage.

Grabby Gabby. *Melee weapon attack:* +4 to hit, reach 5 ft, 1 target. *Hit:* the target is grabbed and knocked prone by an object that was grabbed out of their own hand and takes 8 bludgeoning damage.

A Long Rest

She* doesn't need balloons and banners or her picture on a phone case commemorating the blood vessels she popped in labor or the moment she first saw her baby. She doesn't need to make a list of things she needs help with or a gift card for a spa treatment she won't have time to cash in. She doesn't want another cute onesie with a pithy saying or proclamation of love. She doesn't want to be *so* needed, but she knows it's temporary. She's the fighter, the wizard, the rogue, and the cleric and she just came through the biggest battle of her life. She doesn't need to be the hero. She's just doing what needs to be done. She needs a long rest.

This chapter isn't for the person who just experienced the miracle of giving birth. She's resting, remember? Pull up a chair, friends. This one's for you. The steadfast adventuring party, the townsfolk, her caregivers, maybe a deity or two if she could use some divine intervention.

In Dungeons & Dragons, a long rest is defined as "a period of extended downtime, at least 8 hours long, during which a character sleeps for at least 6 hours and performs no more than 2 hours of light activity, such as reading, talking, eating, or standing watch." Sounds dreamy, doesn't it?

As soon as my D&D character takes the first point of damage, I start asking the DM when we are going to rest. The fantasy me is a bit of a defeatist. Our conversation goes something like this:

> **ME:** Ow, that hurt. Can we rest?
>
> **DM:** Combat just started.
>
> **ME:** But we could probably just walk away, right? I think I saw a nice clearing not too far from here. Let's set up camp!
>
> **DM:** You can't just walk away. You're engaged in combat.
>
> **ME:** The rogue looks sleepy. We should rest.
>
> **DM:** The rogue is fine. The rogue is attacking and doesn't want to rest.
>
> **ME:** Is that true, Rogue? Doesn't a warm bed roll and bowl of pudding sound yummy?

---

* Just a note to recognize and appreciate that not all birthing parents identify as female. As mentioned in my prologue, there are many walks of life to parenting. This chapter uses female-gendered terms in relation to my personal cisgendered experience.

DM: Get back here and fight!
ME: Medic! Can I get a cleric! Someone give me a healing word!

Your party's fighter is best when they're at full hit points. Sure, they could probably still effectively wield a short sword, but the wizard will be so worried about how much damage the goblins are doing to their party member, they won't be able to concentrate on their spells. (It's me. I'm the wizard.) Point is, no one looks after each other better than a D&D party. We take care of our fictional friends better than society looks after new moms.

In the postpartum world, long rests simply don't exist, or if they do, only the very well-resourced can take advantage. Everyone tasked with caring for a newborn will be exhausted. But once that baby enters the world, the person who birthed it takes a back seat as all eyes turn to the newborn's survival. And they should. Babies aren't exactly go-getters. I've never seen one cross a street solo or place an Instacart order. They're just kind of . . . there, and yet it truly does take a village to look after them. But where is the mother's village? Who is taking care of her? After enduring forty weeks of pregnancy, the physicality of giving birth, and the emotional and physical postpartum stress, shouldn't someone be tending to her needs?

Let's talk about labor. The physical work and the mental load. The messy, overwhelming, excruciating, emotional toll on a woman's mind and body when a baby exits her body. We do a lot of things right in the US, but taking care of new mothers isn't one of them. In Mexico, women are "quarantined" for a period of forty days, during which time she is closely cared for with a special diet, rest, and recuperation so that she may return to her pre-pregnancy spirit. In Japan, post-birth, the mother and child return to the mother's family home or village so that other family members can care for the baby and allow the new mom time to rest and relax. In Germany, new moms are forbidden from working for eight weeks and encouraged to stay in bed and heal. A midwife will visit daily for the first ten days to provide help with recovery, feeding, and emotional support. The US ranks last in maternal care out of eleven developed countries due to its lack of maternal care providers, high maternal mortality rate, and no guarantee of paid parental leave in the postpartum period. Paid parental leave laws vary by state in the US, so it's not unusual for the person who just gave birth to have to return to work before their body has physically healed.

Now, I know what you're thinking: *Adapting to a new baby is hard for any caregiver, regardless of if they gave birth.* Fathers, partners, adoptive parents, and stepparents are not immune to the strains and stresses of keeping a tiny human alive, fueled by nothing but questionable casseroles, anxiety, and sheer willpower. That's absolutely true. But no one else grew another human inside their body, carried it around for nine months, and then expelled said human from their body. Babies don't *misty step* their way out of wombs and into their cribs and if you didn't know that I'm gonna need you to stop reading this book and go find another one. Preferably one with the words "miracle of" and "childbirth" in the title and without a stork on the cover. I assure you, that bird's got nothing to do with it.

Pregnancy and preparing for a baby are wonderful things. I loved being pregnant, which I thought was just me being a total badass but was more likely the result of all that extra dopamine coursing through my veins. Even though I was a "geriatric woman" of "advanced maternal age," no one told my uterus that. I had a spring in my step and a glow in my cheeks, and I never missed a workout or a meal. (A friend told me the best way to ward off morning sickness was to never get hungry, so I was advanced in my weight class too.) I was literally running circles around my much younger pregnant friends. I quit prenatal yoga because it was too dull. I gave up *my* seat on a bus for a thirty-five-year-old dude with three grocery bags. I was rolling 20s with advantage and inspiration.

It's what came after that was miserable.

Childbirth wreaks havoc on the body, months or even years after the delivery. It hurts when you stand or sit. You're bloated, bruised, and swollen. If you're really blessed, you might be plagued with things like incontinence, hemorrhoids, fainting or dizzy spells, stretch marks, night sweats, itchy skin, and hair loss. Your body is like a broken vase, trying to hold something beautiful, but always springing a leak. Then there's the mental anguish. Postpartum depression and anxiety are not talked about enough and often go untreated. Being home with the baby can be isolating and lonely, even with a baby attached to you. (They're not great company.) The visits end, friends stop calling, and if anyone asks, it's always about the baby, hardly ever the mother. Asking for help feels impossible. Shouldn't you be able to do it all? You're a mother! Aren't you excited and grateful to be taking care of this baby? You're a mother! You must feel so *blessed* and *lucky* to have this healthy baby. *You are a mother!* This is *the most important job you'll ever have.* You can't quit, the pay is terrible, and your boss is totally erratic and has no control over their emotions. Weren't you supposed to get some superpowers by now? It's some epic level psychological warfare.

Give this woman a long rest!

She can't ask for one, lest she appear weak or incompetent. None of her friends asked for help when they had a newborn. None of her family members talked about how difficult it was. Clearly it's just her. *She* is not cut out for this! Doesn't she know how many people desperately want a child? The lengths they would go to be where she is, wearing a giant pair of meshy underwear and crying in the kitchen? How could she have the gall to be so miserable?

Okay, read this part out loud. *No one knows what they're doing.* Not a single parent. Not the first month, and not a decade later. Even if there are moments of awe and amazement and glimmers of hope, it's still hard. Like, *really* hard. There is no shame in admitting that. You are not inferior or incompetent because you don't slide into parenthood like an ooze through a sewer grate. You are honest. And the more you talk about it, the more you normalize these conversations for other parents. There you go helping other people again! See? *You are a mom!*

Twelve hours after the first drop of Pitocin hit my veins (and eleven hours and thirteen minutes after my glorious epidural), my doctor asked me to put down my *Us Weekly* and ice chips so we could talk about next steps. I was only five centimeters dilated, and because my amniotic fluid was dangerously low, she was recommending a C-section. Not my ideal scenario. Those hospital classes barely talked about C-sections, making them seem like mysterious rituals favored by unsavory witches and celebrities who rolled them right into tummy tucks. But it was almost 9:00 p.m. on a Thursday, and if I wanted to be home on my couch in time for the next episode of *Below Deck*, we needed to get this party started. Besides, the sooner he was out of my body, the sooner I could get one of those chocolate milkshakes all my mom friends were raving about. So off I went to the OR to become a mom.

Post-procedure, while the surgeon and my doctor were putting my organs back inside my body and discussing the improvements to the hospital cafeteria, I was shaking and nauseous and trying not to fall asleep while listening to the anesthesiologist tell me about what it was like growing up in New Jersey. I didn't want to be rude, but some of my best friends were from New Jersey. I got it. Someone asked if I wanted to meet my baby. I hadn't even seen him, yet I did not want to meet him. Not like this. I didn't feel good. I wanted to sleep. I was still shaking. Our first encounter should be under better circumstances. Maybe a quiet room with soft lighting with me in the PJs I bought for this occasion. Seeing his mom splayed out on an operating table looking like a seventh-grade biology class experiment would surely leave an impression, right? Even if he could only see twelve inches in front of him. But the mid-surgery shivers must have made it look like I was enthusiastically nodding because seconds later, a freshly swaddled pink baby was placed next to my head.

"Aww," I said before shutting my eyes in attempt to make the room stop spinning.

Did you know a C-section is considered major surgery? Babies don't. They couldn't care less about their mother's gaping open wounds. There's work to be done! You can't drive a car or climb stairs or lift anything over ten pounds for at least two weeks. And postpartum hormones are no joke. They're the ultimate one-uppers. Keep this tiny human alive, with little to no sleep, no instructions, and a broken body, *and then* add a bonus level of ricocheting emotional dips and peaks. "Mommy brain" isn't a cute epithet for moms who can't stop thinking about things like drinking wine out of glasses with the words "Mama's Juice" etched on them or making bento lunches for small people who reject the effort because you failed to hand them their favorite fork. (Since when do they have a favorite fork? Don't worry, they'll let you know.) It's an actual affliction of brain fog and subjective memory loss women experience postpartum.

At my six-week postpartum checkup, I answered the questionnaire designed to signal if you're experiencing any mental health challenges outside of what's considered "normal" or "mild baby blues." I answered each question thoughtfully and honestly, hoping the results would categorize me as "Not great! Let's get this girl some TLC!" At least then I would know the situation was temporary and fixable. My doctor instead classified me as "doing just fine."

"Anxiety is perfectly common, especially with first-time moms," she said. "You have a lot to get used to. But you will. You're doing great."

At least one of us knew that wasn't true. But if this was truly "common" and lots of people who just delivered a baby felt like this, shouldn't we be talking about it?

So here we are, we're talking about it! How can you take care of your most fragile party member? (*Hint:* It's not the baby!) Good question. You get advantage on all helpful skill checks.

Use your *insight* and ask her how she's doing. Is she really fine? Even if she says she is, even if she says she doesn't want to leave the baby, even if it seems like she's doing a great job, you can search out the truth.

Use your *perception* to notice the things you can take care of. Empty the dishwasher, mow the lawn, take the older sibling to the park, heat up the questionable casserole the Meal Train crew left on the porch.

Use your *persuasion* to get her to hand that baby over (assuming you're actually someone she can trust and *you* have good intentions) while she goes for a walk, takes a nap or a long bath, or runs errands.

Use your *arcana* to conjure a house cleaning service, meal delivery service, or postpartum doula. Magic is real, people!

Use your *investigation* to find out her favorite restaurant and brighten her workday with a special lunch. Do some research on the benefits of a working mom so you're ready to drop some stats whenever the guilt over not being home overcomes her.

Use your *performance* to entertain her for a bit. Bring takeout or cook her a meal, hang out in your sweats, and chat it up like you used to before tummy time and cradle cap were part of her vernacular. Know who also enjoy performances? Kids. Give her a hall pass while you stay home with her kids. (This would be a great time to teach them how to play D&D. Leave the dice at home if you're playing with really little kids though!)

Use your *survival* to help her adjust to this new stage of life. Really, she just wants to know she's not alone. Drop her a line once in a while just to say she's awesome and doing great. Keep inviting her to things, even if she's too tired to respond. Recognize it's hard and validate her feelings and help her get help. Bring a gift for *her* and not (just) the baby.

Use your *animal handling* to take care of her pets. Sadly her beloved fur babies might take a (temporary) backseat while she adjusts to life with a newborn. Offer to take Cooper to the park or give Pretty Kitty Blue Eyes a nice brushing and some catnip.

Use your *history* to *make* history, or at least keep a record of it. Take pictures of her with the baby. She might not feel photo ready, but I promise you she's got pictures of everyone else with the baby, and one day she will want to see herself in these moments. (Pretty sure my son thinks he and I didn't meet until he was four years old.)

Use your *acrobatics* to bend over backward for her. Yes, it's cheesy, but it's the most important thing you can do to help! I mean, unless you really are an acrobat, in which case, use those skills to entertain her!

Unconditional Love

Conditions in a D&D game are a temporary effect from things like a spell or an attack that alter a creature or character's capabilities. While your D&D character may occasionally be plagued by a condition like blindness or paralysis as the result of a spell or an attack, a postpartum woman is probably experiencing all fifteen at once. Do unto a new mom as you would your party member.

Blinded: Ever say you were so tired you couldn't see straight? She might not see that smile on your face, but she'll feel all that positive energy in the form of a foot massage.

Charmed: My baby was the cutest baby, hands down. At least until Baby Yoda. Ten years later, when I look at photos of my newborn son I'm like... well... I mean... if you're into elderly frogs. Babies are master charmers, especially when it comes to their mothers, and there is no countering.

Deafened: If only! She might not hear the story about your coworker who got busted for stealing other people's lunches or the dog barking at the UPS delivery guy, because all her auditory effort is trained on the sound of a sleeping baby. It's pure Zen. Better than any ASMR.

Exhaustion: I mean, not to harp on the whole tired thing, but the Nine Hells knows no exhaustion like that of a new mother, especially if she has multiple children at home. Having one baby is hard. Having more than one is like an evil wizard cast *mirror image* on your bassinet and your whole house is filled with tiny, screaming humans. The only way to counter it is time.

Frightened: What's there to be afraid of? Well, let's name a few. Can my baby be carried off by crows? Can an infant drown without being in water? Will my baby forget me while I'm at work? Social media. Global plagues. School fundraisers. Indoor waterparks. Lice. Teaching your kid how to blow their nose....

Grappled: A grappled creature's speed becomes 0. New moms are spiritually at 0 movement thanks to being exhausted, anxious, and too afraid to expose their infants to environmental stimuli like UV rays, insects, and Trader Joe's parking lots. Mothers of more than one child are physically grappled. All the time. There is no save until they grow up and leave the home.

Incapacitated: The incapacitated mother often finds herself existing in a fog, unable to finish sentences, remember why she entered a room, or figure out where she put her coffee cup. (It's in the microwave.)

Invisible: The ultimate attention seekers, infants have the ability to cast *invisibility* on their mothers (and pretty much everyone else) so that they are the only being to behold.

Paralyzed: My exhaustion got to the point where I would have episodes of sleep paralysis, usually when I woke up to my son's cries. I was conscious but unable to speak or move. (At least that's what I told my husband. *Ha!*) It's not uncommon for postpartum women to experience this as it's often brought on by lack of sleep and stress.

Petrified: After birth, the woman's body will indeed be petrified, and we're not talking the "paralyzed by horror" definition. In the real world, she will be mobile, but movement looks like she's slowly being turned into stone and will often be as painful.

Poisoned: The wild ups and downs of hormones post-birth can make a new mom feel physically ill. Headaches, muscle soreness, fever, vomiting—like morning sickness all over again! Except this time, you have a newborn to take care of.

Prone: The only movement for a D&D character rendered prone is to crawl, and even that is too much effort for a new mom. When prone, standing up takes more effort, and not just because there's a giant bag of frozen peas on her lap.

Restrained: In this case, restrained is more of a psionic condition, as the new mother will *feel* like she can't do anything. Can't shower, can't make a meal, can't write thank-you notes, can't call a friend. It's just easier to stay home.

Stunned: The entire experience of parenthood is a real stunner right out of the gate. There is going to be a long period postpartum when everything feels like a giant apocalyptic triage situation. A running toilet, burnt toast, packing a diaper bag—it's all so dramatic! And then there are moms who return to work—whether willingly or because they have no choice—often just weeks after giving birth. Your new-parent coworkers are overwhelmed and tired and probably feeling guilty about not being home with their child. Please don't steal their lunches.

Unconscious: An unconscious D&D creature is unable to move, speak, or be aware of their surroundings. While mobile, functional, and highly attuned to the needs of her newborn, this describes a new mom perfectly. For the next several months, she will be unable to respond to humans other than the ones in her care, perform regular tasks like meal planning and returning texts, or attend social functions. Triple that if she is a single mom.

The Other Five S's

Our child made it six days before both his parents succumbed to a deep, all-encompassing panic spiral. Our beloved bundle was like a blipping fire alarm with a low battery, only neither of us could locate the source to turn it off. Just when we thought we had him down, he'd blip on again. Even when he slept, his tiny fists were clenched, his brow was furrowed, and his face was perpetually caught in a foul odor scrunch of pure disappointment. That was the only time he looked like me. He had two bozos assigned to his caregiving. What a bummer.

Looking back, he was actually a calm, wonderful baby, pretty chill in the grand scheme of things, but we had nothing to compare him to and weren't used to this level of responsibility. We had old, broken senior dogs who required nothing more than a chewable arthritis tablet two times a day and a soft bed. A baby was next level. This was a *human* whom we made and put on this Earth. The least we could do was keep him warm and fed.

But I can't lie—we were scared. Yes, two grown, educated, relatively fit adults who could no doubt outrun and outmaneuver this kid in a battle of, I don't know, assembling IKEA furniture without those useless instructions, were frightened of an itty-bitty baby. What was the point of all those baby prep classes if we didn't feel prepared to even change his clothes without breaking a bone? Babies are bendy creatures, but those arm holes are so tiny! Would it be bad if our baby just wore capes?

One night while I was in the rocker, strapped to a breast pump, trying to squeeze every drop of life-sustaining liquid out of my tired old raisin of a husk, Bart stood before me, handling our half-swaddled nugget like a hot-potato grenade. He had been crying for the last two hours. ("He" could mean Bart or the baby. It's all such a blur, and honestly both are probably accurate.)

"Rock him!" I yelled.

"I've done that for forty-five minutes!" he yelled back.

"Hold him like a football!"

"He hates it!"

"Sing to him!"

"He won't listen!"

"Bounce him? Pat his back? Blow raspberries on his belly? *What do we do?*" But it was no use. Sometimes babies, like their primary caregivers, just gotta wail. When you are six days old, are confused by the world, and have no other means to communicate, it's pretty much all you've got. (And now I feel guilty. The cycle continues.)

Imagine a Navy SEAL who forgot to read the briefing and had no idea how to use a compass parachuting into the jungle on a terrorist-capturing mission. That's what taking care of a newborn feels like (only without the ninja warrior physical fitness). Then as the dawn broke on parenthood day 7 and I was awoken by the cries of a hungry (or wet or gassy or scared?) baby, I reached my exhausted arms like a sightless mama grell toward the shrieking sounds, and my arms returned with a hardcover book. (Much easier to swaddle.) Oh right. One of the many books I never got around to reading. This one was by a doctor proclaiming to have the secret to soothing babies in five easy steps. Whatever. I tossed it over my shoulder.

"Ow," whimpered Bart. He rubbed his left temple and fell back asleep. Possibly unconscious. Oh, how I envied him.

I pulled the actual baby from his bassinet, and while he ate, I retrieved the book because my new favorite hobby was making fun of *doctors* and their *secret sorcery for soothing babies forced to live with common parents*. How dare they take advantage of our fragile emotional states? There is no—wait, did this title promise to sooth a baby in five easy steps? I mean, did it hurt to try?

This unearthed spellbook was called *Happiest Baby on the Block* by the well-known warlock Dr. Harvey Karp. There was indeed a happy-looking baby on the cover, and despite what I've been told, I do judge books by their covers. I skimmed it looking for bulleted lists, diagrams, and secret passwords.

Dr. Karp's schtick is the "5 S's for Soothing Babies." All of the tactics begin with the letter *S* because new parents love alliteration almost as much as they love sleeping babies. Honestly I didn't care if the other *S*'s were "Shouting," "Scaring," "Stilt Walking," "Staring into the Abyss," and "Serving Sociopath Seals Spanakopita on Silver Spoons." He had me at "Soothe," and I was willing to try anything. Apparently, Dr. Karp's teachings have been so revered and well-practiced that hospitals and educators around the world teach them to parents-to-be. (Unfortunately not part of the mega-package I purchased.) His *S*'s are free, easy to remember, and so simple even zombified parents can muster enough vim and vigor to employ them.

Dr. Karp's *S*'s are meant to mimic the experience of being in the womb—basically a baby's portable sensory deprivation tank, where they were warm, fed, and had all their basic needs met. Sounds amazing. Can a new parent get five more *S*'s, please? Dr. Karp is basically the preeminent Dungeon Master for infants. Get this man a streaming show!

I flipped through the book until I came across the list of *S* words.

- Swaddling (not this again)
- Side or Stomach Position (Babies really hate being on their stomachs, but maybe the goal is to give them something new to cry about?)
- Shushing (was already nailing this one)
- Swinging (not what you think, sssssssorry)
- Sucking (Right, Dr. Karp? It does!)

I almost couldn't wait for our sweetest baby to become unnerved so we could try out our new life skills! Fortunately, I only had to wait fourteen minutes.

"Shush!" I shouted at Bart.

"I didn't say anything!"

"Not you—him!"

I quickly read off the relevant parts of the book.

"Hand me a swaddle!" he yelled like a surgeon demanding a clamp.

"Try him on his side!"

"He's out of his swaddle! I repeat! The swaddle did not hold!"

Eventually we got our baby to calm down, but we still weren't sure if Dr. Karp should get the credit. It was pretty exhausting for all of us, but we were willing to give these *S*'s another go. We made lists of the *S* words on Post-it notes and left them all over the house, stuffed in the diaper bags, on the dashboard of the car, and written on the inside of my wrists with Sharpie *Memento* style. We returned to the five *S*'s early and often. My swaddles seldom held, but there was definitely some real-world charm happening.

While D&D players may enjoy a nice soft swaddle and a swing, Dr. Karp's noble tactics could use a little modification for today's modern gamer parent. I'm feeling like he's got the whole newborn thing covered, but what about when babies turn into full-blown kids? I don't want to get too dependent on these skills only to wake up one day and have my tween-aged child tell me he's too big for the football hold. Don't leave me hanging, Dr. Karp! Big kids need soothing too! Back to the Dungeon Masters.

Some of the best DMs have their own tactical *S* words sure to suppress sudden sullen speech and social graces. Also, "*S* word" is just "sword" with an extra space, and DMs definitely have those too. Yep, I'm really onto something here.

Surprise

My kid just loves hiding around corners and jumping out at me. Never gets old. But when *I* do it to him, he gets super unnerved and angry. I call this "taking your own medicine," but psychologists might call it "bad." Whatever.

Surprises can be a powerful parenting tool proven to increase your child's creativity, focus, and overall happiness. Who doesn't want that? Did you ever see a nondescript paper bag in a store with the words "Mystery Bag" written in black marker across it? Best. Marketing. Ever. Oh how I begged my mom to plunk down five bucks and give me the gift of answered burning curiosity. And likely some cheap plastic toys. Never happened. But what did happen was that curiosity ember had a long fuse, like decades long, because I seldom pass up a mystery bag for myself and my child. We've got quite the collection of dirty rocks, ceramic mushrooms, buttons, stickers, fake gems, and bath bombs that might be poisonous and will definitely give you a rash. Can't imagine why my mom didn't think it was worth it. As it turns out, she could have been making my dreams come true while also activating my neural reward pathways. A "pleasant" surprise not only elicits a positive emotional response, but the memory stays with us longer. (But clearly not as long as being *denied* a surprise, because those memories are burned right into the deepest depths of our psyches.) When our brains are filled with happy, surprising memories, there's less space in there to recall the time your primary caregiver sprung out of a pile of reusable grocery bags in the back seat of the family Forester, causing you to toss orange juice into your own face, blinding you for forty-two horrific seconds, and possibly giving you an ear infection. (I resolutely refute that the ear infection and Great Backseat Jump Scare of 2016 were related. But *someone* stopped drinking orange juice after this incident.)

Dungeon Masters are clever little beasts. Not knowing what's happening is *where* the magic happens. I played an aarakocra ranger with an estranged brother who made up terrible lies in an attempt to get me booted from the nest. I spent decades wandering on my own, wondering why he would betray me like that, and pining for the family I left behind. Sad, right? But it was basically two sentences in my backstory. Or so I thought. During one session, the party came across a mysterious stranger in Baldur's Gate (they're all mysterious strangers in Baldur's Gate). We thought it was an ambush for sure. But then the DM described the silhouette—large feathered head; strong, powerful wings; red and orange plumage eerily similar to my own! When I realized who it was, my heart skipped many beats. I even got teary-eyed in real life. (That's the concept of "bleed" again.) We had a heartfelt conversation where my brother confessed his actions were his attempt to drive me away from our parents, who were actually coldhearted defectors constantly putting his life in danger. So moved by our unexpected reunion, the party asked my brother to join us. I got the family I longed for, the DM got a fun NPC to roleplay, and the party finally got a cleric.

Even though I sound like a big campy horror movie villainess of a mom, I do occasionally have some wins. I pulled my kid out of school an hour early once to take him on an ice cream and movie date. For his sixth birthday, a friend employed by the Pokémon Company arranged a tour of their office for my son and his best friend, resulting in 3,846 photos and several giant bags of swag. One Christmas, we flew him all the way to Disney World without telling him where he was going until we got there. At night. At an innocuous hotel. At a park he didn't even know existed. Hours after it had closed and hours before it would reopen. I thought for sure his surprised reaction video would go viral or at least make the grandparents cry, but he just shrugged his shoulders and asked if they had cheesecake. These are the memories he will most remember. At least until he reads my other books.

Sense of Humor

If you can't laugh, you'll cry, and let me tell you, it gets real weird in the house when everyone is crying. I'm the kind of person who laughs in the face of trauma, awkwardness, and crisis. Some of my best material has been inspired by funerals. If you want someone to howl with glee when a first responder calls, put me down as your emergency contact. Except I won't answer because my ringer is always off. After seeing the D&D movie *Honor among Thieves*, my non-D&D playing friends were surprised the most by one thing: D&D was funny.

"Of course it is!" I shouted. "I've been telling you that!"

"But it seems so serious!" they said. "Like knights and dragons and hard-to-pronounce words!"

Dude, for real? It's a *game* where we pretend to be elves and giant oozes. Sometimes in space. How is that *not* funny? While an outsider might not think your D&D game should be nominated for an Emmy, institutional knowledge, player dynamics, and inside jokes are exactly what *you* love about your group. The same is true for parenting. It's all institutional knowledge and inside jokes. Your family lore will be the stuff of legend. Made-up holidays, mispronounced words, unintentional nicknames for relatives that become standard issue for generations to come. (This is how my dad is now known in most circles as Gekky.) You and your partner/friends in parenthood are going to be in the trenches together. There will be mistakes. There will be a million illnesses you didn't even know existed. *There will be poop.* First order of business: try laughing it off. (The situation, not the poop. You're going to need an enzyme-based stain remover for that.) It's a great lesson for your kid too. Laughter is not just the best medicine; it's mage armor for the soul.

Structure

Have you ever seen a parent just drop what they're doing, grab their toddler, and bolt? That's because it's naptime. You could be mid-conversation with a parent when they see their kid stifle a yawn, and they're gone. Nap schedules are not to be trifled with! Not ever! There is no more sacred a routine than the one around a sleep schedule. Long and short rests are how your D&D character heals up, and a sleeping child is how the parents find their Zen. Sleep training saved me, not just because it taught my son how to self-soothe and fall asleep on his own, but because it provided a schedule (even the illusion of one) for the day. If I could just hold on until 10:00 a.m., 1:00 p.m., 4:00 p.m., and 7:00 p.m., we would be golden.

Structure is a great tool for Dungeon Masters too. It's what holds those beautiful worlds they imagine together. It's why the DM knew there was a trap behind that door and not the missing noble you were sent to rescue. It's how they plot and plan and prep and keep track of all the shady deals your warlock goes around making when it's time to collect. Come to think of it, maybe DMs could use a little less structure.

Study

Stop me if you've heard this one before: There once was a novice Dungeon Master who wanted so badly for her players to have a good time that she actually wrote her own adventure, studied it for hours, planned out how every encounter would go, and failed miserably when her players bypassed the inn where their quest-giver was dining and went to the docks to see if they could barter for a boat with some salty old seadogs. Talk about salty. How would they ever be so moved by the mystery of the disappearing senior dogs to be compelled to investigate? They ruined everything!

But did they? Maybe that DM could have found a nice salty seadog to share the plight of the mysteriously disappearing senior dogs, or maybe while bartering for a boat, the party heard whimpering and after an easy Investigation check saw kennels filled with sad dogs through one of the ship's portholes. (Dang, that's pretty good. I might have to revisit that old adventure.) "Study" in this case doesn't mean pull an all-nighter. It's more of a "skim your notes right before the test" tactic. Survey your surroundings, know your audience, and prepare *just enough* to have some key story beats, NPCs, and monsters in your back pocket, but not so much that you railroad yourself and the party into only one possible story that may or may not unfold. (Remember how cool surprises are?)

For parents, studying can mean things like finding a pediatrician, knowing you shouldn't give a newborn popcorn, and learning when to move your child from a rear-facing car seat to a front-facing one. You can study family-friendly brunch spots or the best hikes for kids or the top ten best April Fool's pranks to pull on your child that even their therapist will think are funny. You know the material. Trust your instincts. You really do have them!

Surrender

Ahhh, doesn't that sound nice. Surrender to a hotel in wine country with a pillow-top mattress and room service. How about a spa that smells like lemons and eucalyptus, where you can treat yourself to a fire-and-ice massage? Would you like a highly trained, CPR-certified nanny who is just begging to spend time with your kids to step in and take the wheel? Good thing you're used to the theater of the mind, because these things are figments of our collective imagination. I'm so sorry. (You and my son can bond over how mean I am.)

For such small beings, babies take up a remarkable amount of emotional and physical space. There won't be as much time for folding laundry, scrubbing the shower grout, or recreating the meals from your favorite French chef on YouTube. And that's just fine. (Who scrubs grout anyway? Are we supposed to?) Your kids will one day discover the movie *Frozen*, so you're going to hear these words a lot, but they bear repeating: *Let it go!* Take a cue from Elsa and surrender to your nine-pound overlord. There's a new world order, and it doesn't involve staying on top of clean clothes or home-cooked meals.

Just as a DM doesn't have to conjure every word of a campaign from the depths of their imagination or make up a new stat block for every monster the group may encounter, parents should also take advantage of tools that exist solely to make your life easier. Published adventures are essentially meal prep kits. The ingredients are all there; you just need to add your favorite flavor. If meal delivery is out of scope, say yes when your friends and family offer to bring you food or help with chores. Having been on the giving and receiving end of these favors, I can tell you that it's mutually beneficial. The giver feels like they're truly helping, and the receiver can have the bathroom towels rolled and sorted just like Marie Kondo taught you.

We lose a lot of things in adulthood—a functioning metabolism, skin elasticity, the freedom to wear skinny jeans and side parts without being made fun of by younger generations. Adults also don't get as many opportunities to be surprised (we can spot a tell a mile away), embrace structure (adults are so lame!), lean on our sense of humor (can't you just be serious!), study for fun (PTSD from SATs), and surrender responsibilities (grow up and be an *adult*). The world is full of contradicting mandates! Fortunately, D&D provides a great training ground for grown-ups to do and be all of these things. You'll be fully prepared to respond when the preschool teacher calls to talk about your child's penchant for scaring other children by jumping out of the craft cabinet. (Remember to laugh. But wait until you're off the phone.)

Parenting by the (Rule) Book

So those weekly emails comparing your growing fetus to a piece of fruit aren't giving you the confidence and know-how to master parenting? It's cute, but recognizing when your baby was the size of a kumquat during week 10 of gestation isn't super helpful in determining what kind of cough your child has.

Expectant parents are welcomed into a whole new world where everyone greets you with a commiserating smile, encouragement, and fluency in a brand-new language. It's like your ears have their own subclass, allowing you to process this strange, secret lexicon. How have you gone this long without *meconium* and *effacement* being part of your daily vernacular? You may *hear* it, but that doesn't mean you'll understand it, because there's no *comprehend languages* spell in the real world. They sound like made-up words, after all. Kind of like the fictional worlds and words in your D&D game. But what if I told you that you were already in the advanced parental language arts class thanks to Dungeons & Dragons? Both are composed of a bunch of made-up, hard-to-pronounce words. Svirfneblin. Sternutate. Slaadi. Say what? When learning how to play a game, you have a rulebook and, if you're really lucky, a know-it-all friend who's been there, done that. Fortunately, you are about to get both. The vernacular Venn diagram between the rules of D&D and the rules of parenting overlap more than you think. Let's break things down with terminology you already understand.

Abilities

You can't have "capability" without "ability." There are six abilities in D&D representing a character's mental and physical prowess: Strength, Dexterity, Constitution, Intelligence, Wisdom, and Charisma. Each of these abilities is assigned a number. The higher the number, the more adept you are at a particular skill. An average human score is a 10 or 11, but because this is a fantasy game, scores can be as high as 20 for the highly adept. As a parent, you will definitely be calling on all six of these abilities several times a day, and your ability score will fluctuate more often than a toddler's mood. No dump stats here. You will want a high score in each of these abilities. (More on ability scores in a bit.)

Advantage/Disadvantage

There's no shame in the "taking the easier road" game. You gotta take those wins when you can! The good news is that kids are susceptible to bribes. The bad news is that they can smell desperation a mile away. The best way to enforce a rule or encourage your child to do something they don't love doing is to bundle it with something positive. *Asking your child to do their homework so family game night can begin* is rolling with advantage. *Asking your child to floss their teeth because they have a dentist appointment tomorrow* is rolling with disadvantage.

Area of Effect

Some D&D spells cover an area, allowing them to target several opponents at once. The shapes can be cone, cube, cylinder, line, or sphere. The areas babies can affect are completely out of whack in relation to their scale. First, all their equipment is ginormous and can spread throughout several rooms in the house and into the yard. Toy size peaks around toddler age, with complete mastery coming in the form of a model kitchen better appointed than your own. Once kids are a bit older and mobile, they will leave a trail of clothing, toys, wrappers, and half-eaten cereal bars like a little slug with a short attention span. They may be small, but the reach of their bodily fluids is mighty. You are seldom out of range. Always keep a shield nearby. As they age, their area of effect is less about their gear and more about their psionic powers. For instance, the mood of a tween or teen can impact anyone within a six-mile radius.

Armor Class

Armor class (AC) dictates how hard you or an opponent is to attack. Your *parental* armor class is variable and dependent on a number of things, like the strength of your immune system, level of exhaustion, availability of your adventuring party, patience, and how late you are for a significant event. A child's armor class is also variable but depends mostly on their emotional state, audience, and how badly you need them to do something. Children are excellent negotiators and prey on a sense of urgency. Stumbling four inches onto a patch of soft grass can be a travesty for a small human and result in a successful "attack." A bathtub full of hatching tarantulas crashing through the rafters and into their bowl of nonorganic boxed mac and cheese while they're watching videos of surprised cats may only be a mild inconvenience. Fidget toys, tablets, and being the youngest sibling all boost a child's AC. Armor classes are a crap-shoot, as so much of parenting is, and can also determine the likelihood of you getting hit by an actual crapshoot.

Bag of Holding

This iconic wonderous item, commonly referred to as a diaper bag, is built to hold considerably more than what its exterior would belie. Until your child is around school age, you will seldom be apart from this item, although it may change shape or size. As the child gets older, the bag gets smaller, and in many cases, the child is granted their own wonderous item, a *handy haversack*, that they can take to school or insist you carry as you sprint through three terminals trying to make a connection. *Handy haversacks* are indeed handy, but they quickly lose their luster. Despite its uncanny ability to hold a ridiculous number of items, a *bag of holding* cannot conjure an item out of thin air, which is unfortunate, considering how many times you will forget to pack a change of clothes or your child's favorite stuffy. This is why filling your *bag of holding* with cantrips is key.

Cantrips

Even though these small but useful magic items can be cast without much effort, don't confuse effortless with worthless. Your arsenal of cantrips can be your greatest utility and will grow right along with your baby. Singing a song or reading a favorite book can lull an overstimulated Shrieking Enchanter into passivity. A ring of keys can be enough to distract your dinner companion long enough to get through a meal. Your ability to disappear and reappear from behind a burp cloth by uttering the riveting words "peek-a-boo" is as close to real-life magic you may find. Snacks, finger puppets, small cars or trains, and a stern "mom voice" are also effective cantrips. Never stop learning and perfecting your cadre of cantrips.

Challenge Rating

A challenge rating (CR) is a number representing the difficulty of fighting a monster. The lower the number, the easier the monster will be to take down. Consider your litany of parenting tasks as foes, all with varying degrees of challenge. Some will be simple and straightforward, like picking up your child when they raise their arms to the sky and shout "Up!" Some will be more difficult, like taking actual candy from an actual baby. Let's take a look at a few other common challenges and the experience points they'll net.

- Hosting a sleepover for ten-year-olds at your house.
  Challenge rating: 5 (1,800 XP)
- Hosting a sleepover for five-year-olds at your house.
  Challenge rating: 6 (2,300 XP)
- Outfitting an infant who recently learned to roll over.
  Challenge rating: 7 (2,900 XP)
- Getting a kid to fall asleep after they devoured a bag of sour worms and three juice boxes.
  Challenge rating: 9 (5,000 XP)
- Making a kid wear a jacket and/or pants in the winter.
  Challenge rating: 10 (5,900 XP)
- Enrolling a child in swim lessons before every spot is filled.
  Challenge rating: 12 (8,400 XP)
- Getting a child to finish thank-you notes less than six months from the gift-giving occasion.
  Challenge rating: 13 (10,000 XP)
- Dressing a toddler in something other than pajamas when they are firmly in their "only wears pajamas" phase.
  Challenge rating: 15 (13,000 XP)
- Teaching a child to cover their mouth when sneezing.
  Challenge rating: 16 (15,000 XP)
- Resisting the urge to embarrass your child, feign an illness, or call an Uber to make your escape while chaperoning a school trip.
  Challenge rating: 18 (20,000 XP)
- Finding a reliable, available, and affordable babysitter your kids love who also has their own car.
  Challenge rating: 21 (33,000 XP)
- Teaching a child how to tie their shoes.
  Challenge rating: 24 (62,000 XP)
- Teaching a child how to blow their nose.
  Challenge rating: 30 (155,000 XP)

Character Sheet

This essential doc is a record of your child's achievements, milestones, and stats. This can be in the form of an artfully arranged scrapbook, hard copies of after-visit summaries from your pediatrician organized by year in a filing cabinet, or a folder full of artwork made with puffed rice and glitter glue you'll donate to their alma mater's library after they receive the National Medal of Arts.

Class

Now, we can't expect a baby to get a job! (Wait, can we?) Just like in D&D, your child's class is so much more than a profession. It's who they are meant to be or are becoming. To know their class is to know your child. Perhaps you're seeing hints of these well-known party members in your little hero.

FIGHTER

A fighter in your D&D party is often the fearless leader. A fighter *at* a party is probably getting kicked out. Sometimes referred to as "strong-willed" or "determined," kid fighters aren't necessarily pugnacious bullies. They have opinions, and they're not afraid to share them—even adults have a hard time doing that. As frustrating as it might be to debate everything from why we brush our teeth to a reasonable curfew for a twelve-year-old, fighters don't always use their power for quibbling. They can often be found looking out for the little guy or fighting for social causes, and that's very noble. Always up for exploring new surroundings, whether it be the compost bin, the fenced-off area behind the playground, or mom's makeup bag, curious fighters pose a flight risk. You'll need sturdy reinforcements to corral them during those early years.

ROGUE

Parents of rogues often find themselves screaming, "How long have you been standing there?!" Like their party counterparts, this kid class excels in stealth and cunning innovation, which comes in handy if you're walking into a movie late or accidentally locked your keys in the car. Hope you like childproofing! Be creative, because they'll figure out that safety latch in no time. "Off-limits" equals utopia. They are masters at hide-and-seek, but if they're hiding, prepare for the game to last for hours. They're always one step ahead of you while also being right behind you.

WIZARD

Sweet spellcasting children with their heads always in a book! (Yeah, I might be a little biased.) While they are inclined toward studious endeavors, don't confuse bookish with bucolic. You know how much those wizards enjoy their fireballs, right? And let us take a moment to reflect on some iconic wizard friends like Tasha of ye hideous laughter, who may or may not have a history of bringing hordes of demon friends to a party; the powerful mage Mordenkainen and his multiverse of monsters; and then there's that power-hungry thirst trap, the infamous lich Vecna, just itching to rule the world and get his own *Stranger Things* spin-off.

CLERIC

Don't stop at STEM for your little cleric; they need a STEAM track to cultivate their artistic side. Clerics are a versatile bunch and enjoy tinkering with code as much as they like doodling with crayons. These are the kids who are most likely to write and illustrate a best-selling children's book about believing in yourself and eschew traditional publishers in favor of starting their own press so they can publish other inspirational tomes written from the POV of up-and-coming deities. Loyal and protective, clerics will come home crying because they accidentally stepped on a crack and fear they may have broken their mother's back. The world deserves more cleric children.

BARBARIAN

Almost every child is multi-classed as a barbarian. While I love having at least one in my D&D party, it's not quite as much fun when a bar-baby's rage is directed at you. Is it really necessary to explode at the person helping you zip up your jacket or pouring milk onto your cereal, or asking you calmly and kindly to please stop rubbing glue into the cat's fur? Nine Hells has no fury like a bar-baby being denied a donut-and-cotton-candy panini or—worse—skipping a nap. Bar-babies rage early and often. Seek cover.

RANGER

The wild child of the bunch, the ranger is the kid at the playground climbing *up* the slide, standing on top of the tree house, scaling telephone poles, or running straight into the arms of danger. Ranger children collect spiders in mason jars and cry uncontrollably when they don't survive. They bond with the crows in their backyard, who return the affection by leaving their handler lost earrings and the bones of other animals. They can be happily sustained on a diet of potting soil and hemp milk. When they grow up, they'll spend their summers as river guides and their winters leading skijoring expeditions in Tajikistan. On the plus side, you'll save a fortune on shoes because they haven't owned any since they were a few months old.

Combat Round

The amount of time it will take for you and your child to call a truce or concede.

Critical Hit

A critical hit in D&D is when you roll a natural twenty on the d20 die. Even though you have as good of a chance of rolling a 20 as you do a 3 or a 13, a 20 feels incredibly rare and is cause to celebrate! There will be a lot of critical hits for your family, like:

- Your baby sleeping through the night
- Arriving at a destination less than twenty-five minutes late
- Potty training
- Correctly diagnosing your child's illness
- Actually having unexpired medication in the cabinet to treat said illness
- Getting your kid to try a new food
- Being known as the fun house with the best snacks
- Having an unbiased adult comment on how well-mannered your child is
- Helping them wash their hair without someone ending up in tears
- Being able to help with their math homework
- Hiding the note from their teacher that says they clearly need extra help with their math homework

Dungeon Master

The arbiter of the rules, the creator of worlds, the comforter of ails, the spinner of yarns! That's you, parents!

Encounter

Any number of scenes throughout the day that comprise your daily adventure is an encounter. These can take place in parks, in doctor's offices, at grocery stores, or on the couch. Each encounter will have some level of difficulty and fall into one of two categories: combat and noncombat. Reading books together = non-combat. Turning off the tablet because it's time to go to bed = combat.

Hit Points

Your hit points (HP) numerically represent your physical and mental health. The higher the number, the harder you will be to hit. The lower the number, the more likely you are a new parent. Babies have more hit points than you think. Toddlers lie about how many they have if they think it will serve their needs. Tweens and teens are much more susceptible to psychic attacks although they'll act like they're numb to them.

Initiative

In D&D, initiative is the order in which turns are taken in combat. It is determined by rolling a d20 and adding your Dexterity modifier. In parenting, the youngest child goes first. Always. Literally, *every single time*, no matter what. No one cares who goes next.

Long Rest

Ha! You wish. Like *find a genie and ask them for a wish* spell. Then use that wish spell to catch some uninterrupted *Z*'s. Enjoy!

Nonplayer Characters

Commonly referred to as NPCs, these are the creatures—friend and foe—who your child will interact with. Good NPCs are neighbors, close friends who want to be addressed as "Auntie" and "Uncle," babysitters, teachers, grand-parents, the friendly clerk at the grocery store who always gives your kid a fist bump, family pets, and stuffed animals. Less good NPCs are the kid at daycare who always has a runny nose, a hypercompetitive player on an opposing team, and any future crush who breaks your kid's heart. How dare they?

Saving Throw

A saving throw is your D&D character's attempt to resist the effects of something negative happening. As a parent you will make several saving throws every day. You don't just get to make them for yourself—you're also looking out for your kid, who is probably too young to be handling dice. Reminding your child to wash their hands after using the bathroom, shielding them from a crushing news story, and not succumbing to pressure to coach a lacrosse team will all require a saving throw. There is no save against your child's aforementioned future broken heart, sadly.

Short Rest

A limited amount of time, usually while the child is at school or napping, dedicated to mundane tasks like getting a long-overdue oil change, doing your taxes, finally getting that hernia checked out, and a million other undertakings now considered resting.

Sneak Attack

Unlike D&D, where only the rogue has this feature, all kids are proficient with this ability. Always be on guard! From faking a fever, to hoarding Oreos under their pillow, to blaming that massive rip in the screen door on the cat, the player always gets played. Your best defense is remembering all the shifty maneuvers *you* pulled as a kid and staying one step ahead! Figuratively, of course. You'll be much too tired to actually keep up.

Skill

Each ability covers a wide range of skills you or your D&D character can become practiced in. You don't need to be proficient in all of them, but knowing how they apply to everyday life will help you decide which ones deserve your limited energy supply.

ATHLETICS

For many years, you'll be your child's favorite playmate. Limber up. It's inflatable-body-bubble blindfolded roller derby time!

ACROBATICS

Bart once dove over the kitchen island and three counter stools to save our toddler, who was seconds away from going headfirst through the cat gate and down the basement stairs. Kids attract danger with the speed of a thousand quicklings.

SLEIGHT OF HAND

Kids, especially babies and toddlers, get really attached to inappropriate objects like house keys, scissors, or another person's hair. These objects must be removed from said child without the child noticing they are being taken away. I have become quite masterful at this skill thanks to the years of stuffing my face with my son's Halloween candy without him noticing all the orange and brown wrappers that fall out of my sleeves. Perhaps the most difficult task is removing an item from underneath a sleeping child's pillow and replacing it with a new item like money. These will all require some serious sleight of hand.

STEALTH

Successfully exiting the Tomb of Horrors is like walking out your front door and feeling a cool summer breeze on your cheeks compared to sneaking out of a baby's bedroom after they fall asleep. There is nothing louder than the popping sound of old joints trying to roll off a beanbag chair and stand upright. Stealth is also required when it comes to tossing out the pencil eraser heads and dried-up slime acquired from six years of birthday party goody bags and folders full of kindergarten art after realizing your kid's artistic abilities might not be as innate as you thought. A toy that hasn't gotten any love in years will suddenly be more in demand than a Cabbage Patch Kid in 1983.

ARCANA

This magical must-have of a skill doesn't just refer to the ability to manipulate reality by way of magical spells (which you'll totally be able to do); it's your ability to recall things like the unsolicited yet practical advice that stranger in the grocery store gave you about colic, a tactic your parents employed that worked on you, or literally anything from those prep classes. Arcana is also useful when being asked to locate a soccer cleat minutes before you're set to pull out of the driveway and head to the game. If only you had a *mage hand*.

HISTORY

All parents are well-versed in history. In fact, as soon as you become a mother or father, you begin most of your sentences with "Back in my day. . . ." It's true that experience is the best teacher. It's also true that history repeats itself, so, you know, maybe call your mom and apologize.

INVESTIGATION

Inquiring minds need to know! Enrolling in kindergarten, putting together a crib, summer camp registration, and getting tickets to see *PAW Patrol Live!* all require proficiency in this inquisitive skill.

NATURE

When I was nine, my parents took my brother and me to Florida. It was the middle of June, and to keep cool, we spent nine hours straight in a swimming pool. This was before parents were taught about sunscreen. I thought the freckles spreading across my nose were cute until they turned into blisters and I lost seven layers of youthful skin on the plane ride home. Clearly my parents were not proficient in the Nature skill, but parents who are know the difference between a hairy woodpecker and a downy woodpecker and why DEET is an important ingredient in bug spray, and they will always be armed with chlorine dioxide tablets and carabiner clips. These are great people to bring on vacation.

RELIGION

Because sometimes you just have to give it up to a higher power.

ANIMAL HANDLING

Carrying your dog's poo around the neighborhood in a plastic bag can desensitize you to what you'll be carrying around in the palms of your hands. Kids love animals and will almost always try to handle them, so even if you're not a friend of the four-legged fur babies, you'll probably encounter some along your journey. Roddy the classroom hamster needs a sitter during spring break. You free?

INSIGHT

Did you write on the wall with this Sharpie? What did you just say to me? Do you have homework tonight? Master this skill and they won't even bother trying to come up with excuses.

MEDICINE

Sometimes a kiss does make it better. When it doesn't, you'll need lots of other options.

PERCEPTION

Did you just roll your eyes at me, young lady? No need to ask. She totally did. Your kids will be convinced you *do* have eyes in the back of your head (tell them it's from an old wizard's curse) because parenting grants you a heightened sense of perception. It's a blessing and a curse, as you'll start noticing danger in places you never saw before (*see*: fruit bowl on kitchen counter). Kids have selective perception, like noticing when you duck behind a garbage can to yank a wedgie out of your butt crack, but they can't tell when their pants are on backward.

SURVIVAL

It's the eye of the rakshasa. Remember how you cared for a tiny human when you were sleep-deprived and fighting hourly panic attacks? Yep, you're definitely proficient in survival.

DECEPTION

My mom told me she had to take a bite of my desserts first to make sure they weren't poisonous. I have used the ol' "It's spicy" trick when I didn't want to share my own food. Kids and compliance don't always go hand in hand, so sometimes a little well-intentioned deception is necessary.

INTIMIDATION

It has been said that never in the history of parenthood has a car actually "turned around" due to the poor behavior of the children riding in it. And yet this empty threat reined in a generation of kids who now employ their own brand of bravado when disciplining their own offspring. Roll high enough, and you won't even need to list the consequences.

PERFORMANCE

Parenting comes with an automatic bard multi-class. It's hard to be entertaining when you're tired all the time and mourning your discretionary income, yet it's just one more thing we do for our kids. Parents require lots of yarn spinning, song singing, and general merrymaking. It's a good thing that as D&D fans, you're already skilled in games of make-believe.

PERSUASION

Persuasion is possibly your most useful skill. Parenting is all about the fine art of cajoling someone into doing something and making it seem like their idea. Kind of like Dungeon Mastering. You'll be involved in daily arbitrations from getting a tiny human to eat breakfast, to getting them to not wear shorts to school in the middle of winter, to getting them to bed on time. It's exhausting, but if you've got the goods in this skill, the hours you save negotiating can be put toward napping.

Spell Slots

The number of times you can tell your child to do something, *anything*, before you totally lose your cool and need a short rest.

See that, young wizard? Your D&D studies have already prepared you for the big stuff. Just gloss right over those other glossaries. One more tip, though? If you do google "meconium," don't look at the images.

Quiz: What Is Your Parenting Class?

There are a lot of choices to make in a D&D game, and that can feel a tad overwhelming to new players. One of the first decisions made is what your character class will be. A brave, brawny fighter? A studious, strategic wizard? A charming but biting bard? How do you really know what suits you best when you have never donned an adventurer's travel clothes? You might be asking yourself the same question with regard to parenting. How do you know what type of parent you'll be if you've never parented before? And before you say "But I have a cat—I know how to nurture," let me say this: I love animals more than I love most humans. I too am an excellent and nurturing fur-baby mom, and yes, some of those skills will translate, but sadly, it's different. No matter how hard I tried, kids just don't respond well to crate training. If my beloved malamute ever sat down with my beloved human child, their conversation would go something like this:

> **HUMAN CHILD**: Let me get this straight. She barely made enough money to cover her mortgage, but you got acupuncture treatments for your arthritis?
>
> **CANINE CHILD**: And doggy massage once a week. But hydrotherapy was my favorite. It was amazing.
>
> **HUMAN CHILD**: We don't even have Band-Aids in the house.
>
> **CANINE CHILD**: I once pooped in an elevator. I was a good dog!
>
> **HUMAN CHILD**: MOM!

Do you *need* to know your parenting class before you officially report for newborn duty? It's not like your pediatrician will make you defend your choice with empirical data and a robust bibliography (in which this book better be included). As with most of parenting, there will be some on-the-job training, but if you're looking to glean a little insight into how you *might* be as a parent, take a look at your fantasy life. *Who* you play may inform *how* you play.

1. You are enjoying a lovely day at the park with your baby and fellow families when suddenly the sky goes dark and a flock of stirges swoops down from above. They're heading straight for your customized, ultralight, convertible, wind-proof, rain-resistant, all-terrain, aluminum-frame, fleece-lined, walking, jogging, trail-running, urban-exploring stroller with the SPF 100 canopy! Do you:
    a. Tell everyone to take cover, toss your 548-piece first-aid kit to the most competent parent, and roll up your sleeves.

   b. Grab a stirge from the sky and bite its head off, Ozzy Osbourne style.

   c. Use the stroller (grudgingly) as a shield and rue your decision to pass up the LED light-up, foil-wraparound, pop-up scarecrow add-on.

   d. Throw Goldfish crackers on the soccer field as a diversionary tactic, giving everyone time to bolt.

   e. Write a strongly worded email to the parks department encouraging them to finally do something about this swooping beast situation.

2. You are receiving unsolicited advice about your parenting choices. Whom do you prefer to hear it from?

   a. Two smartly dressed teenagers and a glossy pamphlet.

   b. Your kickboxing instructor.

   c. A keynote speaker at your weekly charity event.

   d. Hopefully you'll never know because they were smart enough not to show their face.

   e. A book. Even this one. Gosh, aren't books just the greatest?

3. Your kid gets real sassy in public and starts causing a scene. People are watching! How do you react?

   a. Sit on the ground so you can look at them deep in the soul and ask if they need a hug.

   b. Pick them up surfboard style and remove them from the situation swiftly.

   c. Hold your action until you get home and then take away their favorite toy, telling them it hurts you more than it hurts them.

   d. Hold them *gently* by the triceps, fake a smile, and warn them through clenched teeth about what will happen if they don't stop embarrassing you in public.

   e. Doesn't matter how you react because it's not how you thought you would react. What matters is that you're now sitting in your car, sobbing, and listening to a Brené Brown audiobook.

4. After months of begging you to sign them up, your kid hates Ultimate Frisbee and wants to quit after one class. What do you say?

   a. "Being a part of a team is one of life's greatest blessings. Keep trying. I believe in you."

   b. "I told you Ultimate Frisbee was *lame*! How about we try something with more physical contact, like rugby?"

   c. "You made an oath to your team, your coach, and me. You will persevere."

d. "No bigs. I'll tell the coach you broke your wrist practicing and convince him to give us a refund."

e. "Child, you come from a long line of object-hurling prodigies. This is your destiny. Abracadabra!"

5. Your house will be known as:

   a. A Zen sanctuary filled with comfort food and floor pillows. Please join us for ashtanga yoga Mondays after school.

   b. What happens at my house stays at my house.

   c. The home featured on Netflix's *The Home Edit*! Please help yourself to any of the snacks found in the clear plastic containers, but heavens help those who mix the barley millet chips with the organic vegan hemp rice cakes.

   d. If anyone can figure out where I live, I'll let you know.

   e. A realm of tinkering and thinking. Need help with your homework? Looking for your next great read? Want to blow some stuff up in the backyard? Come on over!

6. Your parenting mantra can best be summed up as:

   a. Karma is a bitch.

   b. What doesn't kill you makes you stronger.

   c. Hell hath no fury like a parent scorned.

   d. It's only a crime if you get caught. Wait, what were we talking about?

   e. It's magic, baby. Pure magic.

7. Your single greatest skill as a parent is:

   a. Being a source of comfort and always knowing the right thing to say.

   b. Being a fierce protector of my child while teaching them to stand up for themself.

   c. My fair and consistent approach, which provides the stability and boundaries kids need.

   d. Always staying one step ahead of my kids. You can't trick a trickster!

   e. My wealth of knowledge. Bring on the Common Core math and book reports!

Results

Mostly *a*'s: You're a Cleric!

Congratulations on being a human Swiss Army knife! Whether by brawn or divine intervention, you provide endless utility to your family. A fierce protector and loyal confidant, you are as comforting as a *Price Is Right* rerun and a saltine cracker on a sick day.

Mostly *b*'s: You're a Fighter!

Stand back! No, not you—everyone else. You get the job done and probably hold a high-ranking position in your school's PTA. A dedicated advocate, as the name implies, you will never stop going to bat for your family—a lesson that little biter from preschool learned the hard way.

Mostly *c*'s: You're a Paladin!

When the going gets tough (and it will), the going goes to you. Your unwavering dedication and ability to keep calm in the face of colic make you an ideal partner. Monsters don't stand a chance when you're around. Not only can you suss them out from a mile away, but you'll also make them regret ever taking up with the dust bunnies under the bed—if you let them live long enough.

Mostly *d*'s: You're a Rogue!

There is one spot left at the Montessori preschool, and *it will be yours*. That is, if the admissions board knows what's good for them. You don't have many parent friends but only because they've never seen you. Like literally *seen* you. Do you even exist? You do have many talents, like sneaking in and out of the nursery, getting your toddler to eat that pasta made from chickpeas, and getting out of chaperoning a school trip. Good thing, because you'd never pass the background check.

Mostly *e*'s: You're a Wizard!

A self-proclaimed expert in the parenting world, you've read all the books and studied all the strategies. You've spent hours on your birth plan and see no reason why it couldn't be followed. While some people might see you as quiet and haughty, just *try you* and see what happens. Is it getting hot in here, or is that a flaming sphere in your pocket? As a parent, you're calm but sensitive, clever but reserved, studious but sagely. All the kids come to you for advice and book recs.

Know Thy Game, Know Thy Player

A Storyteller, an Explorer, and a Power Gamer all walk into a tavern. The bartender knows exactly what kind of drink each favors and plops it onto the bar before they ask for it. Before the Power Gamer asks what the specials are, the bartender places a plate of garlic-crusted roast rack of lamb in front of them. Their favorite! The Explorer asks what the quickest route to Luskan is, and without missing a beat, the bartender hands over a fully drawn map marked with not just the quickest route but two alternate routes, just in case of suspected ambush. The bartender has heard the Storyteller's yarn about that one time they single-handedly took down a charmed aboleth and, instead of refuting it, corroborates it. How does the bartender do this? They work for tips. They also happen to be a Dungeon Master and understand the fine art of catering to different player styles.

Allegedly when I was four years old, I was jealous of my older brother because he got to go to school and I had to stay home, play with my toys, watch game shows on TV, and take naps. So unfair. *Allegedly* I had had it with this gross injustice and took my hostility out on my brother's lunch. My brother *hated* condiments, especially mustard, so I *allegedly* squirted the yellow stuff all over the stupid fried ham sandwich and Fritos my mom had packed for him. *Allegedly* that act didn't fill the void not attending school left in my heart, so I *allegedly* continued my vandalism spree by squirting mustard on the six pork chops my mom was prepping for dinner, on the countertops, inside the coffee maker, on cabinets, in glasses, on walls, across the refrigerator, inside the phone book, and on the seat of everyone's dining chair except the one I sat in. *Allegedly* the person who did this wrote SHELLY across the countertops. Perhaps proving her readiness to attend school? Who knows? Not me, because decades after this unsolved mystery occurred, no one, especially me, has ever copped to it.

"Then who did it?" my mom asked, eyes darting around a kitchen that looked like a scene from the Big Bird + *Dexter* crossover we never knew we needed.

I looked her straight in the eye and with all the confidence of a highly trained and overly practiced Miss America contestant said, "The Mustard Monster."

Allegedly the way I said it was quite creepy.

"The Mustard Monster?" my mom repeated. "The Mustard Monster came into our house, ruined your brother's lunch, and used up all the mustard by writing *your* name across our kitchen?"

"And smashed two tomatoes and threw them in the garbage," I added. Accuse me of defacing a kitchen with a condiment, but don't say I'm not proud of my *alleged* work.

"Oh. I didn't see that," she said. "Thank you for pointing that out."

"I did," I said, with my confident mouth and dead eyes. Time to double down. "I saw him do it. He came to the back door and told me to unlock it. You were in the shower, so I did."

"You let the Mustard Monster in?" my mom yelled. Then, realizing what she was getting mad about, she stopped. "Wait, what?"

And then my mom was doubly angry. Not only was her youngest child a creepy, lying vandal, but she clearly had no street smarts. Who lets a monster in the house just because they asked? That did seem like a lapse in judgment. Maybe she should have sent me to school just to feel safer around the house. But what did she expect me to do? Stop a monster? I was four!

My mom told me that because I was the one who let the Mustard Monster in, I had to clean the kitchen. Also, I was grounded from watching my afternoon game shows. She was much too busy trying to figure out what to make someone who only ate three things for lunch *and* dinner. She kept mumbling something about what she was going to do with me and how unbelievable I was, which obviously I took as a compliment. You know what else was unbelievable? My ability to stay cool and collected in the face of a destructive foe hell-bent on destroying our home. I was a hero! She was lucky he only made it through the kitchen before running out of mustard.

The Mustard Monster remains an icon in our family. His tale gets bandied about at least three times a year, more now that I'm a parent with my own potential Mustard Monster. Because Mustard Monster was so well received, I created a whole adventuring party for him: Red Monster, Bee Monster, and, my favorite, Monster with the Glasses. All of these friends were much less destructive than the Mustard Monster, but my mom was still on high alert whenever I talked about them "coming over." She didn't fear her daughter's penchant for imaginary monster friends or care that the neighbors could see me on the front porch "talking" to them. She worried I would fly into another sibling rivalry–induced rage and smear applesauce in the sheets or Miracle Whip on the windowpanes.

Perhaps if my mother had been a Dungeon Master (and she would have been a great one), she would have recognized I was displaying characteristics of a common player archetype and instead of grounding me would have leaned into my strengths and parented accordingly. (I totally should have been grounded.) Just like a family, a D&D table is made up of a variety of personality and play types. Dungeons & Dragons is a game built for everyone, and a skilled DM will be able to recognize individual player styles and know how to adapt the game to keep everyone happy and engaged. Sounds like a lot of work, right? Just you wait!

You as a parent will witness a lot of different personalities. (Sometimes from the same kid, sometimes minutes apart!) Fortunately, one dominant personality type begins to emerge, and kids can be cast into paradigms similar to those of D&D players. Every kid is unique (yes, yours is the best), but understanding you child's "play style" will help you find the right parenting tools to meet their needs and set them up for future success. See if any of these archetypes remind you of anyone you know.

The Storyteller

Storytellers show up to session zero with eighteen pages of backstory no one asked for. They're always looking for ways to push the narrative forward and finding a plot hook in the seemingly inane. Maybe I'm biased, but I think Storytellers are pretty darn cool, even those who dabble in the condiment arts.

My son falls into this category. The first time I heard the word "fabulist" was from his preschool teacher. He came home almost daily with stories about classroom happenings. Once he ate two pounds of uncooked macaroni meant for an art project. A kid stole his nap blanket, flushed it down the toilet, and flooded the whole school. Sweet Eleanor, an advanced crawler, got stuck on top of a ride-on hippo, and he had to set her free. His greatest tale of all time was when his poop set off the fire alarms and the whole school had to evacuate. Kids are, you know, kind of gross, but I didn't think my kid was emergency dispatch levels of gross. We thought it was strange he was involved in so many incidents and yet not a single report was filed or phone call made. Shouldn't the teachers mention the debaucherous antics of our son and his peers at pickup?

"Hi! Your son is out of Pull-Ups, he made this baby frog out of clay, and he's been laundering lunch money in the dramatic play center. Thanks!" Part of me was concerned. Was our child suffering from Munchausen syndrome or some strange version of toddler FOMO? Or was he a raconteur in the making? (Definitely the latter.) Turns out the teachers *did* mention these things. *To the parents of the children they actually happened to.* Another kid ate the uncooked macaroni. The bathroom flooded because someone flushed a rubber glove. Eleanor *fell asleep* on the ride-on hippo, and his five-alarm bowel movement was coincidentally and unfortunately timed with a planned fire drill.

But what's not to love about a kid who invents elaborate, albeit fictionalized, stories? "Fab" is right there in "fabulist." It's safe to say you won't be bored parenting a Storyteller.

Storytellers like: An audience. Be willing and receptive patrons to give them an outlet.

Storytellers need: A different voice for every stuffed animal, and lots of unstructured downtime to explore, create, and wonder. And you'll want to find them a D&D group, obviously.

Engage them by: Playing! Imaginative play (basically D&D without the dice and rules) when they're young, and board, card, and roleplaying games when they're older. Indulge their flights of fancy. You're raising future writers, poets, and Dungeon Masters, and the world will thank you.

The Instigator

The first time I played D&D with Bart, I hated him. Okay, I should clarify—I hated *his character.* He was playing a kenku rogue named Holden Cawfield, inspired in name by a well-known literary character and actions by the little jerk crow duo Heckle and Jeckle. Holden was constantly causing unnecessary trouble. Picking random fights with NPCs, deliberately chasing dead ends, insisting on searching for secret doors when we all knew *there weren't going to be any secret doors! Stop wasting our time, man!* Once, after searching a room and finding nothing, instead of just moving on to the next room, this pesky birdman knocked over a bookshelf just for shits and giggles! I was so irritated by this character; I couldn't help but question the guy who brought him to life.

"Why'd you do that?" I asked.

"I couldn't help it," he answered. "That's how Holden does things."

"Well, you should pick up all those books," I said. "And offer to pay for the damage you caused to the bookcase!"

Bart's not *that* annoying in real life. He was playing Holden true to his character's personality. A DM today might have even handed out Inspiration—a reward given to a player for exactly this reason granting the player advantage on attacks, saving throws, or ability checks.

Bart was clearly the player type known as the Instigator. Some people love playing alongside Instigators. They're not just there to destroy property and cause unnecessary drama. They take creative and fun risks. They don't let things get stale or fall into a lull. When the party can't decide where to go or what to do, they'll take control. I've heard Dungeon Masters praise these archetypes because they're constantly "pushing story." If by "story" you mean "my buttons," then yes, praise be. Give it up for the Instigators.

The Instigator child is exactly the person cast in the stories of my son's imagination. Like their heroic counterparts, they can be prone to rash decisions without thinking through the consequences and get bored quickly. (Hey, Eleanor, maybe don't climb a ride-on hippo so close to naptime, 'kay?) They are also natural-born leaders and innovators with curious minds. What *would* happen if someone put dog food in their little brother's cereal bowl? Would the car look cooler with purple polka dots drawn on the hood? *Can* you paint over Sharpie? Sometimes referred to as "strong-willed" or "spirited," Instigator kids question everything and learn by testing limits. It's exciting to raise an independent thinker! You should be proud. No need to worry about them falling prey to peer pressure and trends. They're the trailblazers other kids want to emulate.

Instigators like: Debates, power struggles, and sentences that start with "What if . . ."

Instigators need: Patience, a sense of mastery, and childproofing. Like Holden Cawfield, Instigator children will knock over anything not secured to a wall.

Engage them by: Letting them see for themselves. In some cases that might mean going against every parenting instinct you have. But if you've told them it's going to rain and they refuse to wear a raincoat to school, they get to sit in a cold classroom with damp socks for six hours. It might have been a poor choice, but it was *their* choice, and that's what matters.

The Explorer

Dora was on to something! Exploration is one of three pillars of D&D, so in a sense everyone who plays the game dabbles in this archetype. In fact, a lot of DMs probably fall into this category too, especially those who enjoy home-brewing their own campaign elements. To be considered a true Explorer one must be bright-eyed and bushy-tailed and ready to take on the world, real or imagined. When harnessed properly, Explorers can provide wonderful inspiration for DMs because they're so curious about the setting around them. What fruit does the merchant have stocked at the market and is it native to this town? What's on the other side of those mountains? That longshoreman giving the party the side eye? What's *his* story? Explorers are natural improvisers and encourage everyone at the table to see the game with an inquisitive eye.

Explorer children are similarly analytical and curious. Their first words are likely "Hey, Siri!" and their first question "Why?" Research shows that when someone has an honest curiosity about something, they learn more, learn quicker, and learn better. It may seem like common sense, but remember that when you are on hour eleven of fielding relentless inquiries.

True to their name, Explorers love to travel and discover new worlds IRL or fantastical. They are filled with facts and trivia and relish the chance to share it. Sure they risk being billed as know-it-alls and their curiosity could be construed as nosy, but you don't want to thwart that probing spirit. Scolding them for asking too many questions now could dampen their curiosity later. Questions and theorizing are a natural part of life. Explorer kids and players are how we end up with guinea pigs for mounts (more on that later) and spells being cast out of the wizard's butt (no more on that later—you're welcome).

Explorers like: An environment rich with possibility and open-ended engagement.

Explorers need: Answers. Teach them how to be resourceful so you don't have to be their go-to solver. Stimulation and provocation. To you it might be a basket filled with buttons and toilet-paper rolls. To an Explorer it becomes a five-star hotel for bugs.

Engage them by: Asking their opinion and how they came to that conclusion.

The Watcher

Two weeks before kindergarten started, some resourceful moms scheduled a meet-and-greet at the school playground for incoming parents and kids to get to know each other. Most kids were immediately drawn to play alongside or with each other, except for one girl who spent the afternoon on a bench with her mom, watching the madness ensue. I assumed she was shy and feeling overwhelmed, and honestly, *same, girl*. Kindergartners have the same play style as a pack of inebriated kobolds engaged in a tavern brawl. I encouraged my son to extend a personal invitation to join him on the four-square court, which she politely declined, content to sit on the sidelines and take it all in.

That girl ended up in my son's class, and the day I was invited into the classroom as the Mystery Reader, I noticed her sitting on the farthest corner of the story-time rug. The rest of the class bombarded me with questions like "Why do apricots look like butts?" and "Why doesn't he have any brothers or sisters?" But her hand never went up and her facial expression never changed—not even a hint of a smile, even after I explained my whole apricot-butt doppelganger theory.

A few years later, I picked my son up early for an appointment and arrived right in the middle of recess. There she was again, sitting on the blacktop in front of a box of chalk and a mural in progress. There were purple unicorns and biped felines, and a sentient sunshine cooling off with soft-serve ice cream. While kids with jump ropes mingled with tetherball players and another group played hula-hoop toss, she was head down, working on what looked like two goldfish enjoying a picnic on the shores of a lake where a sea monster with a sunflower body made its home. On the playground around her drama ensued. Sofie tripped Marigold. Tanner and Micah were rifling through contraband *Pokémon* cards. And my kid was remarkably good at shooting three-pointers and celebrating each basket with a different *Fortnite* dance. But she tuned it out, pulling inspiration from what she observed in her travels and filtering it through a lens of idyllic ideation. My son told me she created a chalk masterpiece almost every day. I wish I could have stayed to witness the end result, but adult Watchers don't go over real well on school grounds.

When there are Watchers at the table, Dungeon Masters might feel pressure to find ways to include them in the action. Their observational nature can be misconstrued as shyness or withdrawal. Should you make every NPC develop a fondness for the Watcher so they have someone to talk to? Maybe the party finds a magic item only the Watcher's character can attune to? Or maybe they're perfectly content to hang in the background. "Fun" looks different for everyone.

Some of my most introverted friends are the most social people I know. While they're not always initiating a get-together, they never say no to an invitation and do seem to enjoy the company of their more gregarious counterparts. Are they going to make small talk with strangers or suggest a game of charades? Probably not. Their idea of a good time just looks different from that of a more effusive partygoer. Parents of Watchers can feel the same pressure as DMs to make their nonjoiners join. The other day we hosted some families we met through a recreational sports league. Two of the siblings spent the majority of the night holed up in the basement playing board games by themselves. I overheard their dad say if they wanted cake, they had to "come upstairs and interact with the other guests." They *did* want cake and reluctantly came upstairs to sit a few feet from where the other kids were playing basketball and awkwardly and uncomfortably ate their cake. I completely understand the panic that springs from thinking your kid is not like everyone else's and trying to make them fit in before anyone else notices. If you think there's a reason your child is withdrawn other than their personality type or preferences, definitely look into it further. If not, congratulations! You have a laid-back, chill, and confident kid who doesn't feel the need to conform with social pressures. All kids are skilled observers—how else do babies learn to hold a spoon or point to where their toes are? Not from reading a book! A watchful child can intuit all kinds of things from their astute observations and develop many skills that will serve them well in life. They have a bead on everything going down and will use that info to come up with clever, out-of-the box thinking. (Should have asked a Watcher if that alarm-triggering poop story was true.) They can also be intuitive and excellent judges of character.

As for the little Watcher at my son's school—if you were worrying, don't. She's doing just fine. I was told she has a few close friends and is basically "a famous artist." She'll either grow up to produce Banksy-esque works of art or reality TV shows. Watch and learn.

Watchers like: Doing their own thing and not feeling pressure to do the norm, active environments where they can securely blend in.

Watchers need: Observational opportunities. It's how they process information and build the confidence to join in—*if they want to.*

Engage them by: Participating in an activity you think they would enjoy. When someone they trust is doing something, they're more likely to as well. Having a shared social activity, like watching sports or playing games, is a great way to have a shared experience without too much attention on themselves.

The Rules Lawyer

Rules Lawyers get a bad rap in game because they're the "Actually, it's pronounced *boo-lay*" players. First, is it *boo-lay* or is it *boo-let*? Does anyone really know? Second, it's a made-up creature designed to resemble a failed mating experiment between an armadillo and a snapping turtle. I don't think they care what we call them.

Personally, I would love a Rules Lawyer at my table when I'm DMing so I wouldn't have to spend so much time looking up things like "Does this require an ability check?" and "How important is accuracy when calculating the area of effect on a spell?" Rules lawyering is frowned upon because it's no one's job to micromanage the rules of D&D. The DM is the final arbitrator of the rules, much to the dismay of Rules Lawyers, and yet all the Rules Lawyers I know are always players.

Yes, rules-lawyering children walk among us. On sidewalks. Because *rules*. They like precision and certainty. Don't say "in a few minutes" if you really mean wheels up in about an hour. They will rat out their classmates for not pushing in their chair or sticking their tongue out behind the teacher's back. They will argue a bad pitch in baseball and use forensic evidence to prove they were not in fact tagged and you are still "it." Years ago, when I first began my quest to harness the ancient secrets of Dungeon Masters, I asked one of the lead rules designers how well one should know the game before attempting to be a DM.

"Oh, don't let the rules stop you," he said, which I found odd because this person literally spent all day *writing rules*. "Just jump in and have fun. That's really the only rule that matters."

Well, that's weird. Why would you tell someone not to bother with the very thing you poured so much time and heart and brain power into? Turns out D&D's rules are meant to be a framework, an outline of how things should work. There are "rules as written" and "rules as intended," and ultimately it's up to the DM to decide which works best. (Again, DMs wielding all that power.)

Admittedly it was a bit hard to grasp, as a DM but also as a player. I'm a bit of a goody-goody. I like dos and don'ts. I'm a Storyteller with a Rules Lawyer moon rising. My smaller personal item will not go in the overhead bin. That will go under my seat, along with my jacket, which also does not belong in the overhead bin (at least until everyone in my row has stowed their larger bag). I will not help myself to a beverage refill if it's not included in the price. Don't want my dog to relieve himself on your immaculately manicured lawn? I'll do my best, but please know fifty-pound pit bulls with digestive issues aren't always keen to reason.

The "jump in and have fun" rule is great for Dungeon Masters but a hard pill to swallow for a Rules Lawyer kid. The world can take on a very scary, *Mad Max* postapocalyptic hue if we just forgo rules. In theory, it's great to have a kid who is a stickler for the established ways. Rules will sometimes keep them safe and out of trouble. They shut off their devices after their twenty-five minutes of screen time is up. They brush *and* floss because the dentist told them to. They are polite and well-mannered. It's when the area of effect on their moral compass expands to others that your kid goes from rule abiding to big old tattletale. Someone's messy desk or penchant for profanity is a personal choice and doesn't need to be policed.

To parent a Rules Lawyer is to understand one. (If only there was a rulebook!) Rules Lawyers want three things: consistency, consequences, and control. Meet them where they are. Positively affirm when they follow guidelines while also freeing them from the belief the world will tip off its axis if little Huxley brings outside food into a movie theater. I get it, kid. It's infuriating having to pay fourteen bucks for a small popcorn while Huxley unpacks a charcuterie board curated with all his favorite snacks from his home pantry. It's a fine balance for parents, but don't worry—they'll let you know if you screw it up.

Rules Lawyers like: Enforcing peace and order. Also jury duty.

Rules Lawyers need: Help understanding that rules get broken, sometimes by mistake, and that being perfect isn't just unattainable, but it's not always the economical choice (as Huxley already knows).

Engage them by: Helping them discover their own needs and freeing them from becoming pleasers. Encourage them to color outside of the lines, literally and figuratively, and show they are loved no matter what.

The Power Gamer

Years ago I worked with a guy who was a game designer on a different team. He was on a recon mission to learn more about D&D, so his boss and my boss talked and it was decided he would join our D&D group. This guy, whom we called Sunshine for soon to be obvious and ironic reasons, showed up to his first session and immediately started barking orders, telling us where to stand, which weapons to use, who to target, and who had the worst snacks (guy had a real chip on his shoulder toward *someone's* delicious dry Kashi cereal and plain Greek yogurt). Dude, chill! This is not how we play D&D! First, we talk about our weekends for forty minutes, then the DM spends twenty minutes reminding us of what happened last session, then the rogue and the ranger remember they were supposed to level up their characters, so while they do that, some of us check our email while the others look at cat memes. And then we play D&D, *collaboratively and collectively,* for the remaining twelve minutes.

Guess we weren't his cup of mead, either, because after two sessions he claimed he had everything he needed to know.

Sunshine is known as a Power Gamer, an archetype all about character optimization and strategizing. On the surface, it's not awful to want your heroic self to be the biggest, baddest version of themself. There are so many bits and bobs and knobs to turn in D&D, it's easy to get lost in all the options. But they can also act like our friend Sunshine, who had no regard for the other players or the chemistry of an established group and tried to turn us into his minions of overmanaged tactical destruction instead of trying to understand our vibe.

Power Gamer kids tend to be naturally smart and innately gifted. They are driven to succeed and make their dreams a reality. They are the proprietors of lemonade stands so profitable that the other kids want to purchase franchises. They crave knowledge and mastery and strive to be the best. These are the kids who read books that aren't assigned and do Sudoku for recreation. They are the reason colleges have early decision.

But a Power Gamer's quest for superiority comes with the risk of burnout, anxiety, and depression. Whether due to their own mechanisms or those of their parents, Power Gamer kids can be overengaged and overscheduled. Remember when baseball was a spring sport? Now you too can play year-round if you're willing to pay for the club teams and spend every winter weekend 175 miles from home, holed up in a Days Inn on the other side of the mountain pass waiting to find out if your kid's team advanced to the next tournament bracket. My kid had a basketball game at a YMCA three exits south on I-5 and I was like, "Oh, look, the YMCA flooded. No game today!" (But then I felt guilty, so we went, and the universe rewarded my good parenting by placing a well-stocked Home Goods across the street from the Y.)

A Power Gamer kid's quest for success can be harnessed for good. It's not a bad thing to want to do better. But the risk of serious emotional issues is never worth the reward—even if the reward is a brass rhino bottle opener found in the clearance section at a discount home decor store.

Power Gamers like: Challenges and experiences where they can show their expertise. And trophies. They really like trophies.

Power Gamers need: A change in narrative that puts the emphasis on achievement and mental health rather than winning and losing. It's admirable to want to hone your craft, but not at the expense of missing out on your best friend's birthday party or the joy of spending all day in your pajamas reading comic books.

Engage them by: Getting comfortable with failure—or at least make it a teachable moment and express love and acceptance is unconditional and not tied to success.

The Most Popular Names across the Planes!

Want to give your child a name that matches their heroic personality and all but guarantees a life of legendary adventures that will be revered for generations to come? Try one of these masterwork monikers on for size:

- Tasha
- Mordenkainen
- Tiamat
- Drizzt
- Asmodeus
- Zuggtmoy
- Vecna
- Orcus
- Soth
- Strahd
- Iggwilv
- Minsc
- Boo
- Jarlaxle
- Bigby
- Bahamut
- Runara
- Xanathar

Don't see anything you like? Want to stick with a more classic traditional name? Grandpa going to be mad if you break a six-generation streak of Zebulons? Not a problem. You can give just about any name some Forgotten Realms flavor by adding a well-placed, completely unnatural apostrophe and some additional consonants. Here are some examples.

Regular Real-World Name	Cooler Forgotten-Realms Name
Liam	L'iamm
Olivia	Oh'live'uhh
Levon	Lvvvv'ohn
Omari	O'O'Omar'e'e'e
Noah	Kno'uh
Emily	M'uhhleaig'h
Charlotte	Sharrr'rrllletttee
Zainab	Zaaeknabh
Alejandro	Ah'leihandrow
Elijah	Ee'l'ijjahh

I Think We're Aligned Now

Your child sees someone drop a dollar bill. They pick it up and tuck it into their pocket.

Your child notices another kid crying and rushes over to offer a hug.

Your child hears you say it's time to come inside for dinner, so they look you dead in the eye, shake their head, and say, "Nah, bruh. That's cap." No idea what that means, but my kid is still outside playing, so. . . .

Why does my beloved scion do that? you'll ask yourself several times a day. Who knows? Maybe because you refer them as your scion? I like to think their *alignment* might have something to do with it.

In Dungeons & Dragons, alignment is a simple system describing your character's moral attitude. Think of it as another tool providing a framework for how your character will react to certain situations. There are nine alignments in D&D, each a combination of two factors: morality and societal perspective. Are you a bloodthirsty mercenary who will do anything for power, fame, and riches? Will you break a rule or two if it means helping someone in need? Unlike your D&D character, a child's alignment can waver on the daily and be influenced by external factors like hunger, a scratchy tag on a T-shirt, or seeing another kid win a SpongeBob plushie from a claw machine. No one can be expected to stay true to their own code all the time, right? (Especially if you logged a solid twenty minutes and forty-five bucks on that rigged claw machine.) If you can figure out how your child's moral compass is calibrated, you'll begin to have an idea of how they'll *typically* behave.

Lawful Good Kids

Lawful Good kids are moral and pious and act according to the traditional definition of "good." Sound great, right? Nothing to worry about here! These are stereotypical teacher's pets who ask for donations to the local animal shelter in lieu of birthday gifts. Do *not* litter in their presence. Even by accident. They never cheat at board games and confess to breaking their own curfew, and they will absolutely be honest about your new hair color. Lawful Good kids are not for those with low Wisdom.

Lawful Good kids thrive in: Jury pools, selling engraved bricks to build a food bank in their town, and the Container Store.

Lawful Good kids struggle with: Finding redeeming qualities in reality TV villains, the concept of ghosting, and people who abuse the generosity of Costco samples.

Neutral Good Kids

If you find you've got a good-natured kid who is mostly chill, goes with the flow, and always tries to do the right thing, they probably lean toward the Neutral Good alignment. When they "act out," they do so with such sincere intentions that it's hard to discipline them. My friend's son drew huge Tammy Faye brows and a clown mouth on their dog with a permanent marker because "he didn't look happy." My son tossed my phone in the compost bin because I told him too much screen time was bad and he thought he was helping me out. When my neighbor and her daughter ran into another mom from school at the grocery store, she yelled, "Look, Mommy, there's the lady you don't like!" First comes honesty, then comes tact.

Neutral Good kids thrive in: Situations that can be resolved with rock, paper, scissors; therapy; and low-stakes recreational sports leagues.

Neutral Good kids struggle with: Poorly written laws, coaches who only play the "good" kids, and exact measurements.

Chaotic Good Kids

Chaotic Good kids never saw a picket line they didn't want in on. Give them some markers and a sheet of poster board, and you've got yourself a pithy slogan and a little lobbyist in training. Don't expect them to do what they're told—unless it happens to be the right thing. Today it's getting that gluey mac and cheese removed from the school lunch menu. Tomorrow it's raising awareness for Helping Hands: Monkey Helpers (a very good cause, actually). Chaotic good kids will unionize if left unattended.

Chaotic Good kids thrive in: Court, nonprofits, and any D&D party.
Chaotic Good kids struggle with: Long wait times to talk to an agent, trusting the process, and trying to return a gift without the gift receipt.

Lawful Neutral Kids

A Lawful Neutral kid will crush that shape-sorter game. Who would even try to put a square peg in a round hole? They enforce turn-taking, do not suffer frontsies or backsies in line, and never peek at their birthday presents. Tradition is important to a Lawful Neutral kid, so before you go putting an elf on your shelf, make sure you're committed to the act for the next several years. Abiding by the rules is important, especially if it's their personal code of ethics. "Yo mama" jokes just make them sad.

Lawful Neutral kids thrive in: Martial arts, Euro-style board game clubs, and a creative writing elective to balance their pre-law course load.
Lawful Neutral kids struggle with: Participation trophies, dead weight, and guessing your gift before they give it to you.

Neutral Kids

Neutral kids were likely "born on the cusp" and will definitely have their star chart done at least three times before they turn twenty-one. It will never feel truly representational. Don't ask them to choose sides unless you have three weeks to wait for a decision. They may come across as noncommittal or lacking conviction, but don't get it twisted. They seek to maintain a balance in the universe and will often act on what feels right. Neutral kids' pastimes include garage sales, knowledge checks, and deliberation. Their favorite phrase is "I'm Switzerland."

Neutral kids thrive in: Hearing both sides, giving advice, and writing press releases for their hometown chamber of commerce.
Neutral kids struggle with: Not knowing the exact time of their birth, sports fans who paint their bodies the team's colors, and being asked to rank their favorite anything.

Chaotic Neutral Kids

Chaotic Neutral children were born late and continue playing catch-up their whole lives. They will not wear pants. Or shoes. Or brush their teeth. I mean, *unless they want to*. But they probably won't. They can often be found barefoot in trees or mapping out bogus star charts for Neutral kids. Many Chaotic Neutral kids grow up to become game designers or crowned champion on competitive reality TV shows. They will put on their own oxygen mask first and walk away. They're fun to have at parties as long as you put your breakables in a safe place, and they make lousy emergency contacts.

Chaotic Neutral kids thrive in: Board shorts and a rash guard, #vanlife, and solo sports.
Chaotic Neutral kids struggle with: Mandatory fun, having to fly home for a wedding, and being taken advantage of.

Lawful Evil Kids

Lawful Evil kids have attended every daycare in the city and have the incident reports to prove it. While they may think they're doing the right thing, they also happen to be the arbitrator of what's right and wrong, but not in a "let's make it fun" Dungeon Master sort of way. They hide the lids for Tupperware containers and hang their wet towel over your dry towel. Do not save their childhood art projects. They aren't nostalgic. They don't join clubs; they start them and then disband them when they get too popular. They can be a loyal friend so long as the friend can follow their rules.

Lawful Evil kids thrive in: Only-child families, the 1980s, and mosh pits.
Lawful Evil kids struggle with: Watching other kids open their birthday presents, Presidential Fitness Awards, and goody-goodies.

Neutral Evil Kids

Neutral Evil kids are the source of 99 percent of playground gossip and misinformation. Everything you don't want your kid to find out will be told to them from the mouth of a Neutral Evil child. All babies are born Neutral Evil, but they usually grow out of it around the three-month mark, when their true alignment begins to show. Neutral Evil kids grow up to be source material for the "mean boss" movie trope—the one who makes their underlings work late on Christmas Eve while they dip out to celebrate the holidays alone in their Aspen chalet. But it's all good because the underlings fall in love, save their town, and open a very successful candy cane shop that somehow manages to maintain a healthy revenue stream all year long. So in a way, Neutral Evil kids actually make the world a better place, and wow, that really pisses them off.

Neutral Evil kids thrive in: Competitive anything—the more ruthless the better, cliqués, and paintball arenas.

Neutral Evil kids struggle with: Underdogs, a redemptive arc, and standing still on an escalator.

Chaotic Evil Kids

Chaos happens. While I like to think this alignment cannot wholly and permanently define a kid, it's definitely something all kids dabble in. External forces are strong in this one. Chaotic Evil personalities can manifest because of illness, a dearth of cognitive skills allowing for emotional expression, or someone they thought they could trust betraying them by trying to pass off a grilled cheese when they really wanted cheese melted between two pieces of toast. Chaotic Evil kids are unpredictable and short-tempered. It's usually a temporary state, but it *is* chaotic and it *is* evil, so it will feel like it lasts two decades.

Chaotic Evil kids thrive in: Environments with impressionable minds; getting their own way by means of tantrums, tattling, or threats; and rage rooms.

Chaotic Evil kids struggle with: Restraint, being grounded, garlic, and sunlight.

Hey, You've Got Style!

Gamers love following directions. Toddlers? Eh, not so much. Their daily journey is filled with more unpredictability and misadventure than a 1st level party exploring the Tomb of Horrors. Ever wonder how you will handle blowouts and broken curfews as a parent? I know, it's hard to say when you're not in the moment, but it's even harder *in* the moment. That's when all your best intentions and hypotheticals fly right out the window. It's hard to resist the siren call of screen time and fast food when you're in minute twenty-nine of a hunger-induced meltdown. (*You,* not your child.)

And yet, your parenting style remains an important question. Your doctor may ask, your partner may ask, the grandparents may ask so they will know how exactly to undo all that excellent work you have done in just a few short hours. This trendy phrase won't just feed the constant and steady river of parenting doubt and guilt you'll be wading through; it's the foundation for how your child interacts with and responds to the world from childhood into their adult lives. Their mental health, personality, friends, relationships, career, and future partners can all be impacted by your choice to send them to time-out or activate their "calming plan." So, you know, no bigs. You got this.

But again, how do you learn all the ways you'll colossally and assuredly leave your imprint on another human before the first drop of spittle has evaporated from their chin? And what about the parenting style of your partner? It's not like you caught the eye of that special someone across the room and as you stood a little straighter and wiped the beer foam from your lip you pondered, *I wonder if they're open to boundary-based discipline?* Better to talk about these things early, but not too early. Somewhere between your first coffee date and deciding to take away Mr. Floppy for twenty-four hours.

There are many factors that will guide your parent style:

- **External influences:** How were you parented? Do you like how you turned out?
- **Societal norms:** Regional, religious, neighborhood, and political norms can all play a part in how you parent your progeny, as will your life experiences.

- **Biology:** Your age, mental and physical health, demeanor, and personality can affect your parenting style.
- **Your child:** Get this—they're all different. It might sound good on paper, but you won't know what works and what doesn't until you put it into practice.

Some factors might be instinctual (they say we all have instincts, but I'm waaaaaaaiting . . .), just like how you are probably drawn to certain play styles and classes in a game like D&D. Some therapists believe we gravitate toward characters who are either extensions of ourselves or the exact opposite. I love a messy, impetuous spellcaster who dabbles in the fine art of wild magic because in real life I'm an anxious control freak who will reload the dishwasher *the right way* after my husband loads it. I think the same is true in parenting. We all *want* what's best for our kids. How we execute that plan is the tough part. Sometimes that's the new, improved You 2.0, and sometimes it's a version of yourself you either wish you had or wish you didn't have.

One of the biggest perks of waiting until I was geriatric to have a kid is seeing the fruits of my friends' labors grow up. I saw a permissively parented child turn into a rebellious teenager with a *face tattoo*! I saw the child of a helicopter parent take a gap year before applying to only liberal arts colleges with an undeclared major. I saw an attached parent check their phone incessantly before bailing early on a moms' night out. If you don't know your parenting style or even what a parenting style means, don't worry! It's like gaming. You might hear about a board game that sounds fun, your friends like it, and it has good reviews. But you don't really know until you experience it yourself. If it's a game of D&D, your experience will be greatly impacted by the Dungeon Master's style. Even if you're not a DM yourself, most likely you've noticed there are distinct personality types. Imagine it's you helming an adventuring party. Are you weaving yarns of your own imagination or adding a few unique details to a turnkey published adventure? Will you buff a monster's hit points to add a challenge and build character (buff it too much and they'll all be building new characters, *waka waka!*), or will you scale down the complexity of an encounter because the cleric is sick and the party used all their healing potions in the last session? Does the idea of asteroid spiders running rampant through space excite you? Or do you reach maximum elation from the undiscovered horrors lurking in the mists of Ravenloft? Running a group of heroes through a D&D world filled with trials, obstacles, and foes can't be that different from raising a kid in a world filled with trials, obstacles, and foes, can it?

If Your Dungeon Master Style Is the Adversary . . .

My first Dungeon Master wanted to kill us. He took it very personally when we bested a challenge or defeated a monster.

"Damn it!" he yelled. "What is wrong with my dice? This pack of boneclaws should have done you in by now!"

And when his dice were hot, he'd fist pump the air and shout things like "Oh yeah, that's what I'm talking about! There. Will. Be. Blood."

I thought that's how D&D was supposed to be played. It's us versus them. That was *our* blood he was promising. The DM's job was to unleash wretched, hungry monsters, and if we got away, find a nice big pit to drop us into or lure us into a dead-end alley in Baldur's Gate to face off with a fiendish flesh golem. It wasn't until two years later that I played with a DM who felt very much like a teammate.

"Why are you helping me?" I asked, after he kindly pointed out my wizard could get more enemies in my *cone of cold* if I moved a little to the left. "Why do you want me to move there? Is there a trap? That's a trap!"

"I'm not *against* you," he answered with a laugh. "I want the party to succeed. We're in this together."

It was so weird. A DM who wanted the party to not just survive, but thrive? And add our bits of story to the world he was weaving before us? It was a literal game-changer.

Some players enjoy an adversarial style of gameplay, and that's fine. It's not all bad. Adversarial DMs tend to be well-versed in the rules, which is impressive considering the *Dungeon Master's Guide* has well over two hundred pages of rules and advice printed in a really tiny font. There's not a lot of gray area with adversarial DMs, but if there were, they'd give it stats and make you fight it.

. . . Your Parenting Style Might Be Authoritarian Parenting

Imagine this conversation:

"Because I said so!"

Okay, it's less a conversation and more a mantra, but if those four words make the bells of your heart ring, authoritarian parenting might be right for you. This parenting style is deeply rooted in making rules and ensuring everyone is following them. The parent is the boss, and they don't ask for much input from the child, believing they themselves know what is best. After all, they were a kid once, probably reared by authoritarians, and look at them now! They rule! Punishments will be swift and mandatory because recognizing the consequences of your actions is how you learn.

Authoritarian parenting often equates obedience with love. Probably not a lot of talking it out or rationalization in an authoritarian household. These parents are generally less affectionate than their "slacker" counterparts and more critical if their children do not perform at the expected level.

I don't think anyone can possibly play D&D exactly the way it was written, just as I don't think every kid can follow every rule levied before them. But the authoritarian parent would beg to differ. And I don't want to get in trouble so let's just move on.

WHAT AUTHORITATIVE PARENTS CAN LEARN FROM A DUNGEON MASTER

Every role is important and the best stories are the ones we tell together. Who cares if the player playing the rogue constantly forgets to use their sneak attack ability? Maybe their forgetfulness becomes a fun story hook for their character. D&D is not about the destination. It's the journey and getting there together.

If Your Dungeon Master Style Is Sandbox . . .

Sandbox stories are driven by the players. The DM is there to make sure no one gets a handful of sand in their eye and there are enough toys for everyone. You might think, *Wow, those lucky players! They can literally do anything!* And they can, until the notion of doing literally anything results in analysis paralysis. Again, this is a very common phenomenon, especially with new players and almost always with kids. When faced with endless possibilities, it's impossible to pick a single one. Kind of like eating at a buffet. Me? I'm a grazing *master*. Rows of incongruous foods shrouded under a sneeze guard don't intimidate me. That is, until I met the one that almost took me down. My friends and I went to Las Vegas for my thirtieth birthday, and my friend Vera won $1,000 on a slot machine. To celebrate, she took us all to the Bellagio for breakfast. (Bye-bye, $1,000. Vera barely knew you.) Look, friends, there's a reason my first D&D character was named Astrid *Bellagio*. It was like stepping onto the gumdrop path on a Candy Land board. Cross the Rainbow Trail to the delicate crepes and golden waffles, then off to the Lollipop Mountains for chia pudding and pain au chocolat, then a respite in Molasses Swamp for king crab legs and a chef-stationed omelet bar. Unlike Candy Land, there wasn't a clear place to start. I was overwhelmed thinking about all the delicious options laid out before me (and some so far away I couldn't even see them) and worried I would miss something spectacular if I didn't study every square inch of this carb-tastic masterpiece. I spent a solid fifteen minutes walking the perimeter of the spread, empty plate quaking in my hand, too paranoid to dive in for fear I'd waste precious stomach space on something silly like a biscuit or home fries when I could get those at my local Trader Joe's. But the biscuits here were so fluffy, and there was flavored butter piped fresh and soft from a pastry tube right on to your plate, and warm honey, and OMG were those beignets with caramel dipping sauce? Auhhhhhghghghhg just give me some Frosted Flakes and a cup of OJ and call it good.

Your first go-round with D&D can feel the same way. This is why really good DMs don't put all the toys in the sandbox right away. They start with a few carefully selected choices and gradually add in more advanced options as players gain confidence.

. . . Your Parenting Style Might Be Attachment Parenting

This approach is child-led. Did you read that? I said *child-led*! No offense to babies, but what the heck do they know about leading? I don't see them lifting one finger to contribute to their care and feeding. It's all "*Wah-wah*, hand me that bottle" and "*Wah-wah*, I peed my pants again!" That's a pretty needy and entitled attitude right there.

Attachment parenting requires constant "togetherness" (in case the word "attachment" wasn't obvious enough) from birth to at least the first six weeks, which in my opinion is pretty much the absolute worst time to be around a child. Again, no offense, babies! In these weeks parents practicing attachment parenting—especially mothers—should be highly attuned to the baby's needs and provide constant nurturing. Personally, I'd prefer a *ring of protection* to attune to, but that's just my own bias against bossy babies.

Now in theory you might be thinking, *What's wrong with meeting the needs of your baby? They're helpless newborns, Shelly!* Nothing, okay? Jeez! Even I recognized that to be a big part of the job. But attachment parenting is not for the lower lumbar challenged. Babywearing, co-sleeping, and on-demand breastfeeding are all encouraged to foster a strong emotional connection. Again, it sounds great and natural, but attachment parenting has its drawbacks too, such as limiting development, creating dependence, and putting the onus on the mother to be the primary caregiver. Not fair to the parents.

WHAT ATTACHMENT PARENTS CAN LEARN
FROM A DUNGEON MASTER

Just like gamers, kids will appreciate boundaries. You're not reining in their creativity. On the contrary, you're leveling up their confidence, which in turn fuels their inspiration. Even if you're playing alongside them, it's comforting to know someone is in charge.

If Your Dungeon Master Style Is the Narrator . . .

When someone asks me to describe Dungeons & Dragons, I always say, "It's a collaborative storytelling game." The word "collaborative" gets them stuck every time.

"Sounds . . . fun," they say. "But how do you win?"

"There isn't winning and losing," I explain. "At least not in a traditional sense. Everyone works together to tell a story and accomplish a common goal."

"But what's it about?" they ask. "What is the *story*?"

"Ahhhh," I sigh dramatically, then put on my reading glasses, pop a pipe in the corner of my mouth, and settle into a wingback chair. "That's a great question. The story"—I pause here for dramatic effect—"is created by players and the Dungeon Master. It is wholly unique and only their tale to tell."

And then I watch a single tear bead down their cheek as they proclaim Dungeons & Dragons to be the most beautiful thing in the world.

Yes, it is. I nod and think, *Wow, I should really work in marketing*, and then my boss reminds me I'm on camera and everyone can see me talking to myself and smoking a fake pipe.

Dungeon Masters who identify as narrators are a beautiful amalgamation of all the things we love about D&D and some of the best parts of all the other DM styles. The only rule they truly care about is the rule of cool. Did it look good? Did it make you feel heroic? Will it sound as amazing as it did the first time when we repeat this story 7,837 times over the next five decades? They have their own ideas, sure, but they'll gladly embrace the players' whims if they *fuel the story*. They actually say things like that! *Fuel the story!* Narrators lay the foundation for a truly memorable campaign and help players feel like the legends they were born to become. They will read your backstory, even help you craft it, if you let them. And you better believe that your assassin mother, who left you in Baldur's Gate at the feet of a statue of Bhaal, the god of murder, when you were a baby, is definitely coming back. You won't know when, you won't know where, and you won't even be mad when you find out the god of murder is your new dad because it *fuels the story*.

. . . Then Your Parenting Style Might Be Gentle Parenting

Gentle parenting feels like it originated with faery families in my most favorite D&D setting, the Feywild. It brings together everything I love about stories and D&D: magic, mystery, whimsy, and weird. It's the land of faeries, but also dark and moody. (Exactly how Bart describes me.) Can't we all just get along? Yes, we can in the Feywild!

Described as a compassionate and understanding approach to parenting, gentle parenting fosters positive social-emotional traits and establishes age-appropriate guidelines and boundaries. Sounds delightful, right? This parenting style positions the parent and child as equals with the parent guiding the child into an understanding of why a behavior isn't appropriate and how it might be changed. Gentle parents lead with understanding, not fear. They encourage working together to comprehend and articulate feelings and always explain expectations and consequences if rules are broken.

While some experts say this style can lead to more empathetic, independent, and confident children, others say it could also lead to permissive parenting and letting kids act out without repercussions. It relies heavily on reasoning, and we all know being reasonable isn't a kid's strong suit.

WHAT GENTLE PARENTS CAN LEARN
FROM A DUNGEON MASTER

DMing isn't the easiest job, but there's a lot to love. It's fun, it's exciting, and it's always your turn. There's also a lot of pressure because you feel like everyone's good time is resting on you. Parenting is hard too, obviously, and the pressure can be intense. But both DMs and parents can alleviate some of that by accepting the fact that mistakes will happen, rules will be forgotten, and sometimes you're going to roll a 1. But everything is a teachable moment. We're all doing the best we can, and sometimes just showing up is enough.

If Your Dungeon Master Style Is the Railroader . . .

Collaboration schmollaboration. This Dungeon Master has a tale to tell and cares not for the players going in and messing it all up. Railroading is a term referring to storytelling "on rails," meaning there is very little improvisation and player choices don't necessarily impact the evolution of the plot. Whether they realize it or not, the characters are corralled from one story line to another. I don't think railroading is a hallmark of a bad or evil Dungeon Master. Rather, I think it's a sign of an unconfident or ingénue DM who means well but is propelled by the fear of being a bad host and wasting everyone's time with what they perceive to be underdeveloped off-the-cuff storytelling skills.

Woo-woo, all aboard the Incompetent Express! What DM hasn't felt some form of imposter syndrome? But when does anything in D&D go the way it's "supposed" to? I'm betting one of the biggest reasons more people don't try Dungeon Mastering is a fear of not doing it well. Even the best DMs still question their skills. When I gained enough confidence to DM after my exceptionally terrible debut performance, I picked a published adventure meant for beginners, gave it a cursory read over my morning coffee, and hoped for the best. This time, when the players bolted in a direction I hadn't prepped, I heard my voice confidently say, "That's a commissary!" in response to "What's this over here?" Was there supposed to be a commissary there? Who cares. It was there now. In my mind the quest-giver was in the tavern, but that didn't mean I couldn't move her to the newly built commissary. And the game didn't break. I wasn't carted off to improvisors jail (which, too bad, because it sounds kind of fun).

Years later I learned a bunch of tactics for when your players do the unexpected but you still need them to stick to a plan. If the entrance to the mine shaft won't come to Muhammad, it's okay to drop the entrance right in the center of town and create a stir in front of it with a bunch of townspeople. Move locations around! Make an NPC with information cross their path and do something obvious to make them stop and talk! Don't put so much of the onus on you! Players want to leave their imprint on your world too, so let them fill in some blanks. Not prepping was so liberating! I actually enjoyed the freedom of making things up on the fly and felt inspired by the moves and actions my players were making. My happy DM medium is somewhere between taking a few notes about key locations and story beats and memorizing passages in the *Dungeon Master's Guide* to trick my players into thinking I know what I'm talking about (don't bother, doesn't work). Candy, on the other hand, always wins.

... Then Your Parenting Style Might Be Helicopter Parenting

My happiest childhood memories are of waking up in the summer, grabbing my Walkman, getting on my purple Pony bike, and taking off. I was gone all day, roaming the sidewalks of the West Side of Binghamton, New York; visiting friends; stopping at CVS to read *Tiger Beat*; riding up and down the hills of Floral Park cemetery. I was alone, helmetless, uncontactable. I occasionally popped back home to use the bathroom and swipe a bag of Doritos. Possibly I had the dime in my pocket my mom made me carry in case I needed to hit up a pay phone to call her. As Bryan Adams sang from the cassette whirling in my beloved Walkman, "Those were the best days of our lives."

Obviously, this magical time existed before cell phones, AirPods, and the pervasiveness of helicopter parents. No way are the children of choppers allowed to explore their neighborhoods unattended and unreachable. *I was alone.* At nine years old! Just me and my bike for eight hours a day! I have yet in my life to recapture that freedom.

Coined in the 1980s, the term "helicopter parent" came about because of their tendency to hover over their children, observing and subsequently freaking out over how kids play. *Spoiler:* kids are wild. They swing off monkey bars, run across uneven sidewalks, teeter on curbs, climb *up* slides, and slide *down* ladders. Helicopter parents are *very* involved in their children's lives, not just keeping them safe but removing perceived obstacles, inflating their self-confidence, and exerting a heavy hand over their environment. The end result can lead to offspring labeled as entitled, lazy, and overindulged. Not surprisingly, studies show that parents who practice this mode of parenting often have worse mental health than their counterparts. Makes me glad to be a "geriatric mom" who is too tired and lazy to monitor her child's every move.

That being said, it's hard to resist some of the tenets of helicopter parenting. Every time my son leaves my line of sight, I instinctively shout "Be careful!" When we moved him from his crib to a toddler bed, I bought piles of floor cushions in case he crashed four inches to the ground. I still drop him off and pick him up from school, which is only half a block away, claiming I just need fresh air. The reality is, he's failed every "test" I give him. Apparently, if a stranger in a white van told him there were *Pokémon* cards in the back, he'd "take a look."

Reluctantly, I'll let him walk to the park alone to meet his friends on a beautiful sunny day with nothing but a basketball to protect himself, and I stand on the porch to watch him until he disappears from my line of sight. Maybe once or thirty times, I'll stop what I'm doing, slink down to the park, and watch him and his friends be perfectly safe, and then spend the rest of the night complaining about how I don't have enough alone time. So yes, perhaps I dabble in the helicopter arts. I'm complicated, okay?

It's not as if the children of helicopter parents are incapable of taking care of themselves or lack basic survival and life skills. I'm sure many have grown up to be highly capable members of society. Personally, I'd love having someone follow me around, opening doors, feeding me snacks, and telling me how awesome I am. But having a parent who never let you struggle, fail, or face the consequences of either might make your path to success just a bit more challenging.

WHAT HELICOPTER PARENTS CAN LEARN FROM A DUNGEON MASTER

Overprepping is the nemesis of collaboration, and overprotecting is the nemesis of empowerment. (I just made that up, and I think these Dungeon Master studies are finally rubbing off on me.) There are some occasions when it's okay to do some light railroading, like if you absolutely need your players to get from point A to point B or find an important NPC, or if that secret door is literally right there, and for Pelor's sake, why can't the rogue roll higher than a 3 and find it?! But players want to level up on their own, and they need to experience the world to do so. A little time apart will be good for both of you.

If Your Dungeon Master Style Is the Coach . . .

Probably the most forgiving of all Dungeon Masters is the coach. This is exactly who you want to run your first D&D game. The coach is always ready to welcome you to the table no matter your experience level, which is why coaches are rampant at gaming conventions and your local game store, eagerly volunteering to host D&D games for strangers. Coaches always have satchels full of extra dice, pencils, dog-eared copies of the *Player's Handbook*, and printouts of character sheets in a variety of levels and classes. They probably have a miniature you can borrow to represent your character, and if they think you've grown really attached to it, they'll let you keep it.

Coach DMs love to teach for no other reason than a love of the game. Every time a new player sits at their table, a DM gets another set of dice. I work with a lot of coaches who exemplify daily the desire to share this magical hobby with more people. No one is prouder than they are when your character does something epic or levels up. They are very involved in character development and share in the party's successes.

Don't mistake coach DMs for people who don't care about rules and boundaries. They absolutely do. They just happen to be excellent at reading the room and tailoring the game to suit the needs of their players.

... Then Your Parenting Style Might Be Free-Range Parenting

Remember that mom who let her nine-year-old ride the New York City subway by himself? Free-ranger. Remember hearing about the pair of elementary school–age siblings who walked three blocks home unattended and almost ended up in foster care? Also free-rangers. (Remember to tell my kid that one.) Remember the mom who was too lazy to take her kid to the park to play basketball and he got kidnapped but also got a bunch of cool skins from the *Fortnite* item shop? Not a free-ranger, because free-range kids are much too street smart and probably have a GPS trackable device.

Almost every human being who became a parent in the 1970s and '80s was a free-range parent, and look at how us Gen Xers turned out! Do not confuse "free-range" with "neglectful" or "permissive." Free-rangers are intentional and of the belief that when kids are ready, they should be able to take on more responsibilities, explore the world, and experience the consequences of their actions. Children raised under this philosophy are learning life skills, baby. My brother and I cooked our own chicken tenders and Rice-A-Roni before we hit double digits. We basically could have moved into our own apartment if landlords didn't have rules about renting to nine-year-olds and if we were strong enough to move my brother's bunk bed.

Free-range parents are less likely to overschedule activities, allowing kids to "be kids" and have plenty of free time and unstructured play. They're not just tossed out of the nest to fend for themselves. Independence is gained gradually, instilling confidence in the child along with the desire to rise to challenges. Both sound pretty good to me.

WHAT FREE-RANGE PARENTS CAN LEARN
FROM A DUNGEON MASTER

Think of parenting as one long campaign. There are peaks and valleys, lulls in the story and nonstop action. Your style may change, and that's great. Try them all on and see what works best, and if you come up with your own unique form, that's even better. It's not whether you win or lose; it's how you run the game.

To the Best of Their Ability Scores

In D&D, your Dungeon Master may ask for an ability check to determine how successful a player is at completing an action. If there's a chance of success or failure, the dice will make the call. The DM decides which of the aforementioned abilities is used to complete the action and the Difficulty Class (DC). The higher the number, the harder it will be to succeed.

Your child isn't the only one with unique abilities (although the grandparents will beg to differ). You, as parents, have them too, but you don't need to compare a dice roll to a DC. Your results will be immediately obvious. Is someone in tears? *Failure.* Is someone wearing pants? *Success.*

While a character can choose to do things like kick down a door or sweet-talk Lord Cinderpuff's valet into granting the party access to his boss, parents don't always have that freedom. You *will* need to do things like feed, change, and bathe your child. As imagined, the DCs for these tasks are a moving target, but here are some solid estimates:

- Remembering to purchase nut/gluten/dairy-free, vegan, organic, sustainable, non-GMO cookies for the classroom Valentine's Day party (DC 15)
- Convincing a new babysitter the whole creamed corn in the purse thing was completely out of character for your little nuggets and probably, most likely, an accident (DC 20)
- Sleep training a baby (DC 25)
- Containing your laughter when your kid drops a contextually perfect, mood-appropriate F-bomb in front of their pediatrician (DC 30)

A great way to identify your strengths and, let's say, "areas of improvement" is to think about yourself as a hero you are about to roll up. Sometimes fiction writers use this approach when developing their protagonist's backstory. Perhaps your hero is fluent in Cookie Monster and proficient at four square. Maybe all the other parents in your village revere you because your backpack is always filled with antitoxins, a mess kit, and several sets of traveler's clothes.

Maybe your flaw is gagging at the sight of snot and wiggly teeth because you were bullied in school by a night hag with chronic hay fever and a vitamin C deficiency. Your ideal is to pass on cultural traditions and hold the family together above all else.

Don't worry if you're lacking in some areas. Just like a D&D party, everyone has a role, so you don't have to master them all, assuming your party members can pick up the slack. My son used to say, "Dads are for farting and Moms are for snuggling." I beg to differ, kid. But I do appreciate a good snuggle too.

There are approximately 3,927 abilities needed to excel as a parent. Because I ain't getting paid by the word here, let's just focus on the six represented in Dungeons & Dragons and why you need them.

Ability: Strength

WHAT IT MEASURES: PHYSICAL ABILITY

Let's take a minute to give a steady golf clap for all the pregnant partners out there. Growing a human being inside of your body is not for the weak. It doesn't get easier once that human is outside of your body because you must still carry them *and* all their gear.

The biggest test of your Strength might be defending yourself against babies! Do not underestimate the vigor of these roly-poly, biologically engineered charm mechanisms! While they appear to have the muscle mass of a sourdough starter, they are surprisingly feisty. Babies are basically mimics. Is that a cute sunflower peeking out of a green pail? A butterfly sleeping on a mushroom? A droopy dog in a hard hat? *No!* Those are babies, and they've got ungoverned fists of fury. What they lack in fine motor skills, they make up for in blind, seething rage. The good news is babies aren't very mobile so you can totally outrun them. Teeny-tiny tennis shoes are wasted on the young.

As they grow, a child's desire to use their own body to transport themselves from point A to point B decreases. The bloom of new mobility quickly falls off the rose, and they're back to wanting to be carried. If you do not accept their request for transport, they will find a way into your arms. They are remarkably jumpy. Like flea beetles. My friend Kari is the mom of three, and once when I was trying to have a conversation with her about the difficulties in finding an online stylist who truly *got me*, she spent a good forty-five minutes rebuffing her children's attempts to be in her arms. Finally, one of them climbed up the wall onto the windowsill and leapt onto her back like a rabid grung. I literally screamed. What in the holy hell was happening in this house?

"Get off her!" I yelled. "Can't you see she doesn't want to be touched!"
It was true, but these were also six-year-olds I was screaming at and not a prospective mugger. It was par for the course in that house. Kari laughed it off and went for a thirty-two-mile bike ride. Kari is one strong mother.

Know this: When kids aren't climbing aboard the SS *Brittle Bones*, your arms will still be full. Not just of memories of phantom cuddles and twelve years of school art projects. I'm talking full of *actual, tangible* goods. *Nothing* made for babies and kids is lightweight or easy to move. An infant car seat is heavy. An infant car seat *filled with an actual infant* weighs the same as a platinum gargantuan statue. And it's painful! (The insides of my elbows are wincing in pain just thinking about it!) Formula, jars of baby food, and seventy-nine Elmo board books all stuffed in a diaper bag are real backbreakers. Even your stroller, which will claim to be featherweight, portable, and easy to fold down from a device the size of a space whale to an envelope, will still require superb core Strength so as not to slip several discs trying to shove it into the trunk of your car. You will need to do all of this while holding an infant on one hip and thirteen pounds of garbage in your free hand. Children always confuse their caregivers with waste receptacles. It's weird. Must be a late ocular development thing, because they're always slipping their candy wrappers and fries that fell on the floor into the pockets and palms of their parents. My kid will walk past several garbage cans with a fistful of trash just to hand it to me like he thinks he's doing me a favor.

YOUR STRENGTH ABILITY WILL BE CHECKED WHEN

- Carrying your child like a surfboard out of a department store (along with those ceramic bunny plant hangers too adorable to be left behind)
- Pushing a stroller loaded with humans, luggage, $385 worth of snacks purchased from Hudson News, toys, blankets, electronics, books, and your weary, tired soul from terminal E to terminal A
- Carrying your child *and* the scooter they insisted on bringing to the park back from the park
- Lugging all thirteen bags of groceries plus a sleeping child from the car to the house because you can't leave your sleeping child alone in a car eight feet from the front door
- Trying to stand up after squatting down to offer a piggyback
- Letting your kids use your shoulders as a diving board in a pool
- Six hours of ultimate football on the beach (worth it)

WHEN KIDS WILL CALL ON THEIR STRENGTH ABILITY

- Clutching a fistful of hair and yanking it from the scalp while never dropping eye contact
- Kicking down a child gate
- Seizing the cat's tail
- Refusing to put one arm in a winter coat
- Holding on to a necklace, earring, or facial piercing
- Hitting a sibling, preferably a smaller one, with their favorite truck
- Refusing to let go of an improvised weapon, such as a fireplace poker, broomstick, or their godmother's rare handblown Murano glass vase
- Climbing out of a crib
- Offering the best, most genuine, toasty, snuggly hugs when you least expect one

Ability: Dexterity

WHAT IT MEASURES: ABILITY AND PRECISION

Can you open a bottle of Children's Tylenol while holding a thermometer to a forehead while also stirring milk into a homemade roux? Can you get a toddler to eat an avocado mashed with quinoa paste? Can you really steal a baby's nose? If so, you probably have a high Dexterity score.

A huge part of parenting is being present without being seen—in the literal and figurative sense. It's good for kids to *know* you're there if they need you, but you mustn't be spotted lurking around, because kids need to practice independence, and honestly, if you keep popping up behind mailboxes and garbage cans, it's pretty creepy.

Probably your greatest feat of dexterity will revolve around getting your child to fall and stay asleep. That whole "sleep like a baby" adage is grossly misleading. Getting a baby to sleep is harder than sending my beloved dragon queen, Tiamat, back to the Nine Hells. (But maybe she wants to go back to the depths of hell because she's also a mom who is sick of holding someone else's trash and just needs a break.) And that's not even the *really* hard part! Once the baby is asleep, all the Chaotic Evil inanimate entities across the planes conspire to wake that baby up again. Didn't know the floorboard in the hallway outside of their room creaked? You do now! Does your neighbor's car alarm work? Let's wait for naptime to check. Who needs to clear all the leaves off the deck with a leaf blower? Literally everyone within a fifteen-mile radius.

EXAMPLE USES FOR PARENTS

- Diving across the table to prevent a glass from toppling over
- Opening the battery compartment of a toy with the world's tiniest screwdriver
- Carrying something in both arms while walking down a flight of stairs
- Dipping into your kid's Halloween candy stash without them noticing
- Sneaking a piece of gum into your mouth undetected
- Dodging the minefield of scattered toys across the living room
- Not falling to your knees when a Lego inevitably gets lodged into the sole of your foot

EXAMPLE USES FOR CHILDREN

- Wiggling out of a hold and darting into traffic
- Poking someone right in the eyeball
- Turning into butter because you don't want to leave a place
- Using any piece of playground equipment without dislocating a shoulder
- Walking across the furniture because the floor is 100 percent lava

Ability: Constitution

WHAT IT MEASURES: ENDURANCE

The first few years of parenthood your endurance will take a beating. Daycare, playdates, school, and toddler gyms are all great for socializing, learning, and growing your community, as well as introducing your immune system to more maladies than there are in WebMD's database. Have you ever heard of *strep butt*? I have. You don't want any part of that, trust me. What you *do* want is Children's Motrin, elderberry lozenges, and rubber gloves. Got all the masks I need, thanks.

EXAMPLE USES FOR PARENTS

- Holding your breath for two and half minutes while cleaning up after a blowout
- Sustaining yourself on the dry Cheerios stuck to the high-chair tray and four ounces of apple juice because you were too busy to eat
- Getting out on the basketball court and holding your own against a bunch of eight-year-olds
- Road trips with toddlers

- Parenting during a pandemic
- Narrowly avoiding the norovirus ripping through daycare
- Lying prone in an uncomfortable position because someone is asleep in the crook of your arm and you're in no hurry to move them

EXAMPLE USES FOR CHILDREN

- Eating thirty-five pounds of Easter candy in as many minutes and still wanting pancakes for breakfast
- Spending four hours at a trampoline park and crying when you're told it's time to go
- Allowing—even celebrating—when someone yanks your teeth straight out of your gums
- Getting knocked to the ground repeatedly by the dog's tail

Ability: Intelligence

WHAT IT MEASURES: THE ABILITY TO REASON AND RECALL INFORMATION

Yes, it seems like there's a lot to know, but as my mom liked to remind me, there were no bags of baby carrots in her day. Wait, what? What do baby carrots have to do with Intelligence? Hear me out: I said *baby* carrots. Get it? Okay, for real, I have a point. Our parents didn't have half as many resources that exist today, and they did just fine (yeah, look at you!). And our grandparents had even less, and so on. There were no YouTube videos or Facebook groups or car seat experts to show you how to install your gear and maybe point out how dangerous it was to let your kids ride backward and unrestrained in the back of a cigarette-smoke-filled station wagon, and yet—here we are. My mom always brought up those damn baby carrots after she stopped hosting Thanksgiving dinners for thirty people. She washed, peeled, and chopped *fullsize* carrots to serve on crudité platters, but nowadays they come already bagged, washed, and ready to go. (This was her version of walking to school uphill in a snowstorm.) The fact that there are over 65 million Gen Xers still roaming the planet attests to the fact that much of parenthood is fueled by the whole "Kids are tougher than they seem" philosophy.

Your parenting brain, like your constitution, is going to get a whooping. All that juicy matter that used to be reserved for fun things like reciting the monologue Liam Neeson delivered to his daughter's kidnappers in *Taken*, the words to Young MC's "Bust a Move," and the last name for every core character on *The*

Facts of Life (Ramsey, Warner, Green, Polniaczek, and Garrett, because some of us still got it) will be overrun by things like the *Bubble Guppies* programing schedule, your pediatrician's direct number, and which of the kids in first grade have nut allergies. It's not great dinner party fodder, but at least no one gets left out at the classroom Valentine's party.

EXAMPLE USES FOR PARENTS

- Remembering the names of your kid's friend's parents and teachers
- Telling your child to *stop it right now* . . . with your eyes
- Memorizing your kid's favorite book so you can retell it anytime, anywhere
- Assembling toys
- Keeping track of everyone's schedules and making sure they have appropriate gear, snacks, clothing, and a ride home
- Researching schools and getting on waitlists at least five years in advance
- Getting your baby out of a car seat without turning it upside down

EXAMPLE USES FOR KIDS

- Absorbing lyrics of the worst television theme songs
- Recalling that time four years ago you were late picking them up from school
- Communicating with other kids via acronyms
- Waiting for absolute silence on an airplane before asking what diarrhea is and if you still have it
- Convincing parents of their younger sibling's guilt
- Forging a parent's signature to get out of school

Ability: Wisdom

WHAT IT MEASURES: THE ABILITY TO PERCEIVE AND UNDERSTAND

Wisdom is Intelligence's artsy, kooky, crystal-wearing cousin, and it is key for survival. Yes, you have it! You've heard of mother's or father's intuition, right? (Actually, I have never heard of father's intuition, but I don't want the dads to feel left out.)

Wisdom is why your hips start swaying whenever there's a baby in your arms or you tuck a gourmet candy bar behind a throw pillow a millisecond before your kid walks in the room. Just as your D&D character's gut instinct might tell them that the shiny box marked "treasure" is probably a mimic, a similar divination will guide you on your parenting adventure. Once, on our way to a trampoline park, Bart was driving and our son was chatting away in the back seat. We came to a red light, and for whatever reason I felt compelled to unbuckle my seat belt, dive into the back seat (also using dexterity), find an empty plastic bag, and put it to my sweet child's mouth mere seconds before he tossed his Lunchable. There was not one sign this was going to happen. Even our child was surprised. It was so bizarre and freaky we didn't even talk about it until we pulled into the parking lot and I asked the attendant where the nearest dumpster was.

"How did you know I was going to throw up?" he asked.

"A mother always knows, my sweet child," I answered. Truthfully, I have no idea what possessed me, but it saved me two hundred dollars in car detailing, so I'll always be grateful.

Your wisdom will guide you through some of your toughest moments. When you start to question yourself, you'll hear someone say, "That's your child. You know them the best." Don't panic! That's just your wisdom voice. Consider that your "rule of cool." When the Facebook groups and books on your nightstand and WebMD don't come through, trust your gut. In fact, start with your gut.

WISDOM CHECKS FOR PARENTS

- Anticipating your toddler's next move and cutting them off at the pass
- Seeing an open socket seconds before your kid tries to stick a body part in it
- Knowing when your kid is lying
- Discerning the difference between a healthy glow and an allergic reaction
- Bringing down a fever
- Packing snacks even though your kid swears they're not hungry
- Resisting the pleas to adopt a lop-eared bunny

WISDOM CHECKS FOR KIDS

- Pointing out all the open sockets in your childless uncle's home
- Convincing the cat to act as a pillow while napping on the living room floor
- Knowing you've been caught and when to cut your losses and come clean or find a scapegoat

- Picking up on your strange neighbor's vibes but only mentioning how creepy they are when they're out of earshot

Ability: Charisma

WHAT IT MEASURES: FORCE OF PERSONALITY

My son told me he has high "teacher rizz."

Say what?

"Teacher rizz," he repeated. "Because teachers love me."

Ah, I get it. Cha-*rizz*-ma. Not all of his teachers love him (just got an email proving that), but it's clear my son already understands the power of the sway. Charisma is a skill that serves you well in a D&D game. It's often used as the magic user's spellcasting ability. It can help you win friends and influence enemies. It will help a bard charm a crowd and a rogue win big in a card game. The rizz can't be understated, no cap, and if I rolled high enough on a performance check, that sentence coming from me would sound as cool as it does coming from a fourth grader.

Babies are not as easily won over, and they don't give it up for just anyone. For people who don't even know what a sense of humor is, they remain your most critical audience. And just when you think you've got a fan, it turns out to be gas. Watch out for the brutally honest toddlers. What they gain in vocabulary they lose in tact. They are sharp-tongued and filterless. Once in a Zoom meeting with thirty people, a coworker's daughter popped up on camera and told us we were all stinky. Tough, but fair. If they don't like the looks—or smell—of you, you and everyone within earshot will hear the review. Better work on that rizz score. Charm, persuasion, even a dash of mild intimidation will serve you well.

CHARISMA CHECKS FOR PARENTS

- Rebuffing repeated invitations to join the fundraising committee
- Distracting a child about to get a shot with funny faces and goofy noises
- Getting your kid enrolled in a summer camp even though the registration has been closed for two months
- Replacing your child's beloved hermit crab with another hermit crab before they realize old Mr. Snappymitts passed away
- Befriending the parents who show up late to every baseball game, are kind to the teenage umpires, and drink White Claws out of their Yeti tumblers

CHARISMA CHECKS FOR KIDS

- Walking out of a store with the exact thing your parents insisted they weren't buying
- Telling the waiter it's your birthday so you get a free piece of cake
- Standing up for another kid who is being bullied
- Getting your parents to stop at a fast-food restaurant on the way home from grocery shopping
- Being the class clown
- Negotiating a higher rate for your chores

Moppet Manual: Bewitched Betwixt

These bewitching in-betweeners are caught between two worlds. At once fiercely independent and desperate to prove their societal rank, but also clingy, codependent, and inconsistent. They lure their prey by pretending to be snuggly, helpless imps, when in reality they're actually just lazy. They could get their own tablet charger or pour their own cereal, *but so could you*. Bewitched Betwixts prey on those who once provided care and comfort. They often travel in packs, showing fierce, albeit ephemeral, loyalty to their own kind. Should a fellow Bewitched Betwixt receive any positive affirmation or attention, the other Bewitched Betwixts will become combative and contentious until an equal amount of attention is bequeathed unto them. Several times a day the deity they worship will change.

While easily bribed to stop or start doing something, the Bewitched Betwixt is a fickle beast and cannot be trusted to perform the simplest of tasks with speed or accuracy, or even perform them at all. It is impossible to reason with a Bewitched Betwixt.

➤ **Best Defense:** *Food.* Only offer consumables that are beige, white, or yellow with a high starch content. *Crush.* As much as they like attention, Bewitched Betwixts are highly susceptible to the idea of another Betwixt liking them. Like *liking* them. Telling them someone has a crush on them or, worse, *they* have a crush on someone else will render the Bewitched Betwixt temporarily frightened.

BEWITCHED BETWIXT

Tiny fiend, Lawful Evil

Armor Class 13
Hit Points depends on their mood
Speed 120 ft

STR	DEX	CON	INT	WIS	CHA
4	0	1	2	1	22

Skills Deception +4, Insight +3, Persuasion +4,
Damage Resistances cold, bludgeoning, piercing
Damage Immunities fire, poison
Condition Immunities poisoned
Challenge 12 (35,000 XP)

Shapechanger. The Bewitched Betwixt's appearance can change several times a day. The shape of their face, size, height, weight, voice, and eye color will morph before you.

Minor Mirror Image. Instead of creating three illusory duplicates of themselves, when threatened a Bewitched Betwixt will cast *minor mirror image*, morphing their face into that of your own. Are those *your* eyes rolling in the back of your head? Is that *your* puckery baby lip quivering? Is that your cute, whittie-bittie forehead bunched up with the fury of a thousand angry barracudas? Awww, so sweet! Opponents must succeed on a DC 20 Wisdom saving throw. On a failed save—and let's be clear, *you will fail*—opponents will suffer years of guilt and remorse and a feeling of failure. This condition is unsavable.

Under the Influence. Bewitched Betwixts exist under the false notion that they are unique and original, but they are actually controlled by highly paid demons from another plane who communicate with their subjects through an endless stream of videos. These demons dominate the wardrobe, jokes, and even the kind of water they drink. The spell can only be broken by cutting off all communication with these pervasive demons at the source. It has never been done.

ACTIONS

Mood Swing. Bewitched Betwixt can cast *mood swing* at will as an action *and* a bonus action, even outside of combat. *Mood swings* are invisible and impossible to see coming. Getting hit by a *mood swing* will result in 17 points of emotional damage.

Hangry. Creatures within 30 feet who lack the proper rations or distractions to please a Bewitched Betwixt must succeed on a DC 18 Dexterity saving throw or take 10 (3d6) psychic damage.

BONUS ACTIONS

Humiliation. Several times a day, the Bewitched Betwixt can tap into its intuition and target one or two vulnerable creatures it can sense within 60 feet. The Bewitched Betwixt has the innate ability to sniff out an inopportune moment to do something wildly inappropriate like drop an F-bomb or projectile vomit. Each target must make a DC 16 Dexterity saving throw. On a failed saving throw, the creature takes 7 psychic damage and is overcome with exhaustion.

Kids Play the Darndest Things

Hopefully you're starting to see how parents can learn a lot from Dungeon Masters, but did you know kids can learn a lot from Dungeons & Dragons? I know this because two decades ago I wasn't a fan of D&D or kids, and now I spend most of my days trying to bring the two together.

Gen Alpha kids (born between 2010 and 2024) have a lot of things going for them. They're fully digital, creative, socially and globally conscious, focused on mental health, and entrepreneurial. Pretty awesome, right? But they're also growing up in a world filled with new and emerging challenges. Climate change, social media, food developed in labs, too much screen time, and the occasional pandemic, to name just a few. (Can someone please give these kids a Constitution boost?) My friend who is a family therapist has some good news and bad news. The bad news is that most of her patients are adults working through childhood traumas. The good news is, she has more business than ever! Yeah, didn't make me feel better, either.

Parenting is not just a job; it's the *most important job you'll ever have*. People with the most important jobs probably need someone to help them be successful, right? How would you like an assistant that would almost assuredly support you on your quest to raise well-adjusted, kind, open-minded, tolerant, independent, inclusive, responsible, good-mannered, empathetic, caring, and creative children who also happened to be above average in math, reading, and writing? Time to make like a magic user and step back, parents. Let Dungeons & Dragons take the wagon wheel! Give that child a set of dice and put fate into their own hands—as soon as the dice are no longer a choking hazard, of course. D&D is good for kids!

Perhaps this is not a shocking revelation, as I'm guessing many of you discovered D&D as children and you're pretty much crushing it. Maybe it's a coincidence, but I like to think D&D helped hone some of those positive life skills. As I mentioned, my D&D discovery didn't occur until I was an adult (and yes, I know it shows), and it was because my boss made me. Cute game and all (so I heard), but definitely not for me. A *roleplaying* game? With *pretend characters*? Steeped in *fantasy*? How could an attention-starved, hammy ex-theater major writer with a cadre of imaginary monster besties from childhood find any enjoyment in that? Then I was offered a job in the book publishing department at Wizards of the Coast and was seated mere feet away from *those Dungeons & Dragons people*. Sure, they *looked* normal. They ate regular human food for lunch and spoke about things like *their pets* and *long weekends on the peninsula*, but I kept one ear to the ground listening for the sound of a whetstone on a blade or a mumbled incantation. I always found their weirdo dice in conference rooms, stacked in precarious formations. Mindless distraction while stuck in a boring meeting or a secret symbol to conjure some demented elf lord? (Obviously the latter.) And what was with those strange maps and odd language comprised of unpronounceable words? That seemed unnecessary. Ever hear of a vowel? I mean, we get it. It's a game of pretend. Must everything be so dramatic? Couldn't your little made-up town just be called Fairyville or Scaryunders?

So I faked it for a while, laughing at their inside jokes, pretending I got it when someone called me Shelly Menzoberranzan (I've been called worse), and *ooh*ing and *ahh*ing over the covers of the latest books (the art actually was pretty stunning). But my returned blank stares and cold sweats when asked a question about D&D gave me away. I could only plead spontaneous laryngitis or a phone call from my mom for so long. The jig was up. My boss had this crazy idea that people who got paid to *market* something should know a little about it. What business school did *she* go to? So off I went to my first (and assumed only) D&D game with five other newbies, contemplating what it would be like to have a job that didn't force me to play games for two hours with really nice people.

I'd like to say the rest was history, or at least pretty obvious by now. I fell in love with Dungeons & Dragons, and even writing that sentence feels odd. The story; the freedom; my beautiful elf sorceress, Astrid; my fellow party members— all captivated me that fateful afternoon in a third-floor conference room with a strange map and words I started to comprehend on the whiteboard. I almost burst into tears the first time flames burst from my character's fingertips. *I* did that. My little Astrid incinerated a mini forest of twig blights ready to ambush the party. The real me couldn't figure out a Zippo lighter until college.

The interesting thing about almost every adult I know who loves D&D is that they loved it as a child. Ask them about their first introduction, and they'll take you right back in time. They were around eight or nine, it was summertime, and an older brother or cousin or mysterious teenage friend showed up with a box with a big red dragon and beefy-thighed warrior in hot pants facing off in a blazing epic battle. And those kids didn't know *what* was in that box, only that they loved every piece and parcel of it. Right there in their friend's sunken living room with the teal carpeting and Ring Dings, they became beefy-thighed tween fighters and brainy wizards and sly assassins. Their imaginations ignited, fueled by the promise of never-ending stories and limitless adventure. They're probably still friends with that group, and even if they don't get together on the regular to roll some dice, they never stopped loving the game or those memories.

These are the stories I love. Besides eighties sitcoms, there are very few fandoms in my own life that have this kind of pull. (Now, if I had discovered the Real Housewives when I was a kid, it would be a different story.) I have spent years trying to figure out what it is about D&D that turns curious gamers into fans for life. One thing is clear: It's extra special when you grow up with D&D as a creative outlet and formative social activity. I'm committed—no, *obsessed*—with bringing that 1980s energy to the kids of today. It started when Greg Tito and I interviewed Kade Wells on *Dragon Talk* years ago. At the time, Kade was an English teacher at a Title 1 school outside of Houston. A lifelong D&D fan himself, Kade knew firsthand how the game could have a profound impact on your life.

"D&D saved my life," he often said. "If it weren't for this game, I wouldn't be here."

And if he weren't here, he wouldn't be introducing D&D to kids like him. Kids who otherwise would fall through the cracks in the education system or get written off for being difficult, unruly, and disinterested in learning. So on a whim, Kade started a D&D club, and a bunch of kids joined, many of whom were struggling academically, socially, and/or mentally. Then a bizarre thing happened. These club kids started doing well in their classes and were soon outperforming the rest of their peers and eventually the entire district on standardized tests. How could kids from disparate backgrounds with different experiences and different teachers all improve their test scores at the same time? The only common denominator was Dungeons & Dragons. That's when Kade realized he was onto something and set out to educate the educators about what he calls "the most innovative teaching tool in the world." This has become Kade's life's purpose. And helping him spread the word became mine.

Greg and I interviewed other guests like psychologists Raffael "Doctor B" Boccamazzo and Megan Connell, and Adam Johns and Adam Davis from Game to Grow, a nonprofit dedicated to using games to foster educational, community, and therapeutic growth. All were using tenets of D&D in their practice to help kids and adults with anxiety, depression, ADHD, PTSD, and even autism. This completely blew my mind. Our little game was so much more than entertainment.

I knew there were other teachers like Kade who believed in the power of D&D to excite and engage students in their classrooms but didn't know how to incorporate it. Many of those smarty-pants kids from the 1970s and '80s who were fed a steady diet of rust monsters and spider queens in their youth were now educators. Of course they would jump at the chance to share their favorite hobby with the next generation. D&D was unique. The awareness was high, even before there was a big media vehicle like a major motion picture or animated series. Kids today, like the ones from nearly fifty years ago, were intrigued by the very *idea* of D&D. I pull out a box with a dragon on it, and next thing I know, there are six kids sitting around my kitchen table. I guess just the hint of a dungeon or a dragon is enough.

Then in 2021, I got my chance to put my master plan in action.

Everyone knew D&D innately taught hard skills like math, reading, and writing. That part was obvious (but not to kids, which is also why it's so amazing). But did you know D&D can foster growth in soft skills like empathy, inclusion, collaboration, listening, problem solving, and resilience? I got the green light to work with a curriculum design partner and to test a program creating D&D-inspired activity kits for elementary and middle schools. The curriculum was launched in conjunction with the D&D Afterschool Club Kit—a physical kit providing everything an organizer needed to start a club at their school or library.

The club kits sold out within months, and when I got the initial results for the curriculum, it was like someone cast *psychic scream* on me. My goal was to reach one hundred thousand kids in their classrooms. Thanks to some very dedicated visionary educators, we reached nearly *four million kids* in just a few months.

Four.

Million.

Kids!

It was hard to ignore that real-life magic was happening here. Introducing kids to D&D is like granting them unlimited access to a creative, boundless, friendship-making portal. Probably the biggest surprise was an email I read from a mother who was so moved by the success of this program and wanting to share her love of the game with the next generation of fans that she was ready to abandon the warm, wooly confines of her comfort zone and start the first ever D&D club at her son's elementary school. What an awesome lady!

But wait.

The email was coming from *inside the house.*

My house!

The email . . . was from *me.*

Oh no. What had I done?

I spent so many months convincing other people to bring D&D into their schools that somehow I managed to convince myself. After COVID, kids were behind socially, emotionally, and academically, and they were craving personal interaction. It had been three years since the school allowed afterschool activities. I penned some of my greatest words one afternoon in an email to the principal pitching the idea of a D&D club, including data points, case studies, links to articles, and research studies. I offered up Bart and me to run the games. We'd do it for free, of course. Seconds after hitting send, I regretted it. *She's going to hate the idea! She won't get it! My son will be doomed because everyone will know his mom is one of those weirdo dice-collecting witch nerds.* (I wish.) Worst of all, *I don't want to DM!*

She wrote back six minutes later.

"Sounds good! Please work it out with the PTA."

Oh no.

The PTA definitely wanted a D&D club, especially one run by two dorky parent volunteers. I placed an ad in the school newspaper looking for other parents to help and recruited two more dads—both who played D&D as kids and still loved it (see?). One was extra excited because his daughter and her best friend wanted to join the club. When registration opened, our club filled up in under three minutes and the waitlist shot into the double digits. In a world where enrichment activities include things like fashion design, Ultimate Frisbee, and Japanese lessons, D&D was the invite of the elite.

"What the hell is happening?" Bart asked, thinking back to when he hung out in the elementary school library, hiding his *Player's Handbook* inside a less dorky read, like *Popular Science.* "Schools are actively bringing D&D into the classroom? Kids are publicly talking about it?"

Yes, indeed. Almost daily the PTA would email asking if I found more Dungeon Masters, because there were some *very eager* parents hoping to get their kid passage to Stormwreck Isle. I stopped wearing D&D merch to school because parents would stalk me, offering to pay more or quickly learn how to DM if that meant getting their kid into the club. (Please let the record show that I did not leverage this.) All of a sudden, my D&D-ambivalent child was looking at D&D in a new light. Some of his friends signed up without knowing we (or he) had anything to do with it. They talked about it at lunch when they could have been talking about basketball or YouTube. The friends who were stuck on the waitlist offered bribes in the form of Jolly Ranchers and first-ups in kickball (he did leverage this, even though he had no pull). This frenzy warmed my cold lich heart, imagining kids asking their parents to sign them up because they thought D&D sounded fun. I couldn't help but think how cool it was that one day I would figure into someone's D&D origin story. *When I was in fifth grade, I joined the D&D club started by a couple of nerds. The dad was pretty dorky, but the mom was the greatest human ever to grace this planet. She went on to be a* New York Times *best-selling author and opened a convalescence ranch for senior dogs.*

Of course, all this personal enthusiasm was tempered by an all-consuming terror. It was one thing to tout the benefits associated with kids playing D&D (and yes, our club kits did provide everything I needed), but OMG I was going to be a Dungeon Master. For *kids*. Get out of my head, stupid lunchtime game from a decade ago! I hadn't felt this much anxiety since seeing two pink lines on a pregnancy test. I'd like to say I didn't overprepare, didn't stress-read the *Dragons of Stormwreck Isle* adventure six times and cover every page with color-coded Post-it notes, didn't stay up into the wee hours of the night googling things like "Teaching kids how to read a D&D character sheet" and "How can I get kids to think I'm cool?" But, well, you know me by now. Also, there's no way to get kids to think you're cool. Just thinking that makes you decidedly uncool.

Ready for the character arc you never saw coming? I got excited. I approached Dungeon Mastering with the same pragmatic resignation as I did my due date: Millions of people have done it with even less experience than I had (sending love and support to Tammy and her baby born in a toilet bowl). And I already committed, so either this was happening or we'd be making a sizable donation to the PTA. The thing was, not one of the twelve kids in the club cared how versed I was in 1st level spells or if I knew when to ask for an insight check. They just wanted to play D&D. I knew *enough*. Oh sure, I would get confused and make up a few new rules. I would miscalculate a monster's attack and make an encounter more unbalanced than a football standing on its end, and 95 percent of the time I'd pick up a d10 when I meant to grab a d12 because I'll never tell them apart. I'd forget NPCs names, mispronounce locations, and make up answers when they asked things like "How does sneak attack work?" (Uh, be very quiet as you attack?) and "Why do you sweat so much, lady?" (I have no idea, but I'm guessing it has something to do with middle age). But so what? We had a story, willing heroes, and our imagination. And we had the best time.

It was seeing kids who didn't know each other huddled before school, working out a plan to get from the Sea Caves back to Dragon's Rest. It was the emails we got from parents thanking us because they hadn't seen their kid this excited in years. It was the joy I felt telling them, "Yes, even though you have a ranged weapon, you can absolutely kick that zombie in the face" or, "Wow! Killing an innocent quest-giver sure is a unique tactic for a paladin!"

Playing D&D gave the kids a rare opportunity to be themselves while being other people. They were wildly creative, funny, generous, kind, smart, and adventurous. They tried to tame every creature and turn it into a familiar. They went absolutely *Lord of the Flies* on an NPC who was supposed to be their guide, but I forgot about him until the last session. (Note to self: Kids do not take well to abandonment.) They took *a lot* of bathroom breaks. I overheard one kid tell my son he was lucky because he could play D&D anytime and heard my son sigh and say, "They ask me to play all the time, but I'm pretty busy." The teachers said D&D was spreading like an errant fireball. It was all the kids talked about. Even when they had free choice and access to tablets and laptops, they gathered together on the carpet with their pencils and paper and took off on a storytelling adventure. It was clear which of the students had that DM energy. We let them co-DM, and it was incredible to watch a quiet, reserved kid command the attention of a table of her peers. A couple of them started writing their own adventures. Kade's vision was coming to life in room 302.

I wrote lengthy weekly recaps for parents, but also for me because I didn't want to forget a minute of it. Fortunately I was also capturing best practices for DMing for kids, which as we know by now is basically the same as raising them.

Be Quiet and Listen

No, not the kids. I'm talking to you, parents. The kids were new to D&D *and* me, so I had no knowledge of their play style and very little knowledge of who they were as people. Would they fight everything in their path or try to make friends with every animal-like creature? Would they be shy and respectful to their quest-givers or overconfident and greedy? Would they refer to their character in the third person or fully embody their heroic self with a unique voice and thirty pages of backstory? It took a few sessions to get comfortable, but it soon became obvious what they were into. They liked interacting with creatures. (I had to do a *lot* of voices.) Humans were boring. If a monster didn't attack them or the attack missed, they got angry. Anything even sort of animal-like would be adopted.

A warm-up period is totally normal when playing with a new group. You have to find your rhythm, and that goes double for parenthood. Your newborn is basically a stranger. A really cute one who might even look a bit like you, but a stranger nonetheless. It's totally okay if your warm-up period takes a little longer.

Don't Worry about Milestones

Bart and I split the kids into two groups and started the same adventure at the same time. By week 3 we were in completely different places. It was fun to hear the kids compare what happened and how they handled the same situations, although I got sick of my group asking why the other group got a pet octopus and they didn't. Bart's party moved quicker than we did, maybe because he's a much more experienced DM, but I felt pressure to catch my kids up, maybe to the point of rushing them. One session we never left the shores of Stormwreck Isle. They opted to stay in the very spot where they *just* fought a bunch of zombies. Runara, their quest-giver, was waiting a short distance away at Dragon's Rest with a hot meal, a healing word, and their next cave-dwelling encounter. But the party had different plans. They were determined to build a hut and spend the night. (More on that in a bit.) I knew we would be even further behind the other group, but they were so excited about building a shelter, I told them to go for it. Off they went searching the beach for materials, working on a trap system in case enemies approached, and most importantly talking to each other *in character*, which brought up a lot of interesting on-the-fly backstory work. Had I been too focused on getting us to the next encounter, we would have missed out on what became my favorite session and the moment many of those kids "got" D&D.

Babies start rolling over as early as four months. By six months, most probably have had a few go-arounds. Fun fact: My son never rolled over. Not one time. He went from lying flat on his back to perfecting a step-back 3 in basketball. And guess what happened? Absolutely nothing. Today, at ten years old, I assure you, he *can* roll over—in both directions.

If your niece is potty trained at two years old and your son is three and show-ing no interest, it's all good. There are probably plenty of things your kid can do that evade Little Miss Lavatory. Your doctor will let you know if something needs further analysis, but most kids just move about at their own pace. Mile-stones, like D&D rules, are just there as a guide.

It's Okay to Say No (and Sometimes You Really Should)

My DMing style is what most would call "pushover." I didn't want to thwart creativity or crush spirits, and I wanted to instill the whole idea of being able to do anything. (Yes, I did also really want them to think I was cool.) But I also didn't want the kids to think *I* was the arbiter of failure and success, so I made it very clear that that distinct responsibility belonged to the dice. As the weeks progressed, the kids were getting more comfortable treating me like their submissive babysitter, and the requests became more outlandish and impact-ful. Soon the 1st level wizard wanted to cast 7th level *prismatic spray*. I mean, it *would* be fun to have a rainbow of doom and destruction burst from your fingertips, and far be it from me to deny a child such a simple pleasure. Then the naughty paladins wanted to poison the friendly, innocent inhabitants of Dragon's Rest. Um, okay, that's awful, but maybe a teachable moment? (Thank-fully they rolled low.) And then the party retrieved two lost eggs belonging to a grateful griffon couple who were imprisoned in the hold of a shipwreck. Instead of handing them over, the party decided they wanted to keep one. They would only free the griffons if they acquiesced.

"But those are our children!" the griffons pleaded.

"Well, we're only asking for one," they reasoned.

They had a point, but to "Yes, and . . ." this seemed cruel. "Yes, and you have kidnapped the unborn child of two distraught, potentially dangerous parents who most likely aren't going to let that fly." (See what I did there?) I turned to the volunteer dad who assisted at my table and asked him what I should do. "Is this intimidation? Or persuasion? What do I do, Edward?"

"You could just say no!" he said all incredulously like I hadn't even consid-ered that. (I had not.)

I *could*? Really, Edward? I have the power to tell children they can't take an imaginary egg from an imaginary griffon couple? Okay, I guess I'm still a little green and probably bitter about being bullied by children. *And* Edward. It was definitely *intimidation*, Edward. I suppose the same goes for parenting too?

You're saying I could just tell my kid no? And he'll just go away? Why doesn't Edward just write a little book if he's so parenting savvy?

All right, he had a point. Even though D&D is all about making bold choices and trying anything, there are times when you can say no. Maybe the character isn't strong enough to lift the slab off a sarcophagus or the delusional party thinks they can take on a tarrasque—at 1st level. Think of parenting as a balance between "Yes, and . . ." and "No, but . . ." and steer them in a different direction or find a compromise. Kids gotta push those boundaries and make their demands. But they'll survive. The 1st level party versus the tarrasque will not.

About Those Boundaries

Toddlers are a lot like a curious low-level adventuring party. Where there's a world, there's a sticky hand searching for a something to smash. A clever DM can find ways to keep the party on track if they're not catching hints or pulling at plot threads that aren't going anywhere. As kids start feeling themselves, they want to know what they can and can't get away with. Are toys for throwing at a picture window? Will screaming at the top of their lungs result in a third cake pop? Does this moss-covered rock taste as good as it looks? Yum-yum! Annoying, yes, but also a completely normal part of their development. This big, beautiful world is filled with teachable moments.

Even Heroes Make Mistakes

There I was, a young tabaxi ranger being chased by a stegosaurus through the jungles of Chult. The rest of my party was ahead. I knew this dino could outrun me and would catch the rest of my group mere seconds later unless I took him out first. I was swift and accurate with my bow. They didn't call me Sure Shot Paw Paw Paw for nothing. Without slowing down, I turned around and fired. I had done this move hundreds of times before. Except this time the dice were not impressed. I rolled a 1. Instead of letting me lick my psychic wounds and move on to the next player, the Dungeon Master pressed for details.

"If you rolled a 1, you didn't just miss," she said. "You spectacularly missed. Like shot-yourself-in-the-foot missed. Like arrow-bounced-off-a-tree-and-hit-you-in-the-eye missed. Like tripped-over-a-monkey-brush-vine-and-landed-on-your-little-kitty-face missed. Like—"

I got it. It was an epic miss. *Moving on.*

"Well, what is it?" she asked, relentless. "What happened to you?"
Describing my epic successes was normal. One time I caught a girallon completely by surprise by casting *misty step* to teleport onto his back and stab him
in his neck with my short sword. Another time I kept the party hidden from a
pack of velociraptors with *pass without a trace.* I am usually masterful with the
hunter's mark and longbow. But on this day? Not my time to shine. Must I be
forced to relive it in all its shameful glory?

"Um, so when I reached into my quiver, my bracer got stuck, causing me to
lose my balance and fall down? But I fell into a pile of leaves so, you know, soft
landing."

"Okay, great," the DM said. "So, you're lying there, facedown in a pile of *soft*
but wet, muddy leaves and a rampant dinosaur is coming up behind you."

"Sure, but the leaves must camouflage me a bit. I do tend to favor a flora-and-
fauna-hued wardrobe. I'm sure he just runs right by me."

"Right by you? Let's see." She rolled a d20. "Okay, sure, he doesn't see you,
but when you fell down, you landed on a branch and cut your forehead open.
That's gonna leave a mark."

Oh, it left a mark alright. The mark of a Dungeon Master who exploited bad
dice rolls. Genius! Sure Shot, like my son, was a bit of a fabulist, and whenever
the party found themselves in a town or a tavern, she'd belly up to the bar, re-
galing the townsfolk with another tale that always ended with "and that's how
I got this scar!" "Tall-tale teller" ended up being one of my favorite attributes of
Sure Shot, and I didn't know she had this side until I rolled that 1.

I'm sorry to tell you this, but your child will be disappointed one day. Quite
a few days, really. There is no mage armor or shield in real life to protect them
from setbacks, but you can give them something better: resilience. Teaching
them about self-care, empowerment, helping others, and finding ways to foster
healthy relationships with friends and family is a great way to build this important life skill. Take a lesson from Sure Shot Paw Paw Paw's character sheet.
Failure isn't feared in D&D. It's revered for generations to come.

Fake It Until You Make It

I let my DM guard down when I realized most of the club kids had no idea how
to play D&D. By the time they figured out the real rules, I'd be just a distant
memory of a middle-aged lady mom with pockets full of banana taffy. It was
liberating! I could do whatever I wanted! And as long as I *acted* like I knew what

I was doing, they bought it. Same deal with your newborn. Not only are they new at this whole being a person thing, but they don't have the energy to fight for control. You rule, babies drool.

You're Doing Way Better Than You Think

By the time the club wrapped, there were a few kids who knew how to play better than I did. I'm pretty sure I'll be working for one of them in a decade or so. On the last day of school, when the kids ran out of the building into the arms of summer vacation, my future boss ran past me and doubled back.

"Hi, Shelly," he said. "Thanks for teaching me to play D&D."

And then he was off, which was great, because seeing your Dungeon Master burst out crying on the tetherball court is super awkward. Bart and I worked our butts off on that club, and despite all my worries and anxiety and fear of disappointing them, those kids had fun. Even if they didn't say it explicitly, their parents did. And I could tell by the melancholy vibe on our last day and their lack of eye contact when we handed them their giant swag bags, they were going to miss us.

Trying to do well as a parent is half the battle. No, it's got to be at least three-quarters. Your children will remember decorating the house for holidays and family game nights and how you always let them crack the eggs into the pancake batter (and then spend the next twenty minutes picking out the eggshells). You'll have days when you think you've really messed them up or realizations you're not the parent you thought you'd be or moments when you think you're failing to measure up against someone's arbitrary set of standards. But then you see your child's eyes light up when you pick them up from daycare or see your six-year-old scan the bleachers for you when they're declared safe on first base or see the picture they drew of the two of you holding hands with the caption written in crayon: *I love you.* They'll remember you being there. Showing up for them, like a Dungeon Master shows up for their players, full of nervousness and excitement, ready to watch what they'll do with a world full of possibilities.

Baby Monsters

When my son was a toddler, he called the D&D plastic miniatures depicting various creatures and foes "baby monsters." Regardless of it being a green-eyed spidery beast with fangs or a bug-eyed beholder firing off a death ray, he would see these evil-eyed monsters on Bart's bookshelf and squeal "Babies!" and ask to play with them. That was all fine and cute, because they were tiny and not real, and we created some fun stories starring these guys. But as he got older, I realized some baby monsters were tiny but very real. Baby monsters walk among us. They are spotted in school, on airplanes, and in restaurants. Some might even *live with* you or be invited over for playdates.

Kids go through more phases in a day than the moon goes through in a month. Remember, they are new to this whole "being a person" thing, so words and emotions can be hard to figure out. Fortunately, most phases are short-lived, and some are actually pretty adorable, but when your sweet little child morphs into any of these baby monsters, it's best to know how to contend with them.

Doppelganger

OMG, it's *you*! But smaller! And—no offense—cuter.

I used to think it was a compliment when my mom looked me dead in the eye and said, "I hope you have a child just like you." Aw, Mom, thank you! That's really sweet! You want me to also reap the gestational gifts bequeathed by a child like me? I hope so too. Then I had a child just like me and realized this wasn't a blessing. That woman cursed me.

Think it's easy to defeat yourself in a contest of wills? Guess again. If you truly knew yourself, you'd know how exhausting you are to tangle with. The smaller you could do this all day. Just try them. DNA is truly a monster.

Gibbering Mouther

"Have you seen this YouTube video? How about this one? No, this is the one I wanted you to see. Watch my *Fortnite* dance. Guess what Kayla said to Maya about Mia! Why are they called belly buttons? Do sharks have buttholes? Watch this! Look at me! WATCH THIS!"

And so it goes and goes. Don't bother asking a Gibbering Mouther to take a breath or stop talking. They are incapable of hearing anything other than the sound of their own voice. And don't try to flee. Gibbering Mouthers have an excellent sense of direction in that they can sense whatever direction you're heading and follow. They will always be one step behind and also ahead, brandishing a tablet in your face or giving you a drawing of a rainbow dinosaur for you to frame or telling you how bored they are. You are their best audience. Also their social director. It's a lot, but do try to cherish this time, because they genuinely want to hang out with you. Don't worry. They'll stop talking when they're teenagers.

Boneless

They will not walk out with their heads held high. In fact, some of them won't walk out at all. There is no nuance to this quivering, waffling mess. The name says it all. Children's bones are special. While they're made of the same stuff as yours and mine, they can turn to goo on demand. Usually there is a command like "It's time to leave, let's go," or "No more sugar, you just had cotton candy and a lemonade," or just "No." That's when your upright, bipedal bambino turns into a thirty-two-pound water snake. You can't remove them from situations because the Boneless *are* the situation.

Intellect Devourer

During pregnancy, a woman's body is overtaken by a constant wave of hormones, which cause physiological changes to her brain. These hormones are known as Intellect Devourers. They eventually take the form of your child.

Perhaps you've heard the term "Mom brain" or "Momnesia"? It's no fantasy! Pregnancy (and, sorry to say, parenthood) can cause poor concentration, bad memory, and difficulty focusing on everyday tasks like, I don't know, mothering. Although parents aren't technically incapacitated (at least by the D&D definition), the Intellect Devourer will engage in the most imbalanced battle of the brains, from which they will always emerge victorious. Winner takes the cognitive control and consumes every thought and action of the parent from now until eternity. But they're so cute we hardly mind.

Mimic

Is that a sweet sleeping baby or a holy terror devil demon ripped from the bowels of the Nine Hells? Wake it and find out. No, *you* do it.

Mimics in D&D are notorious, and some might say "Not fair!" (It's me. I'm "some.") Dungeon Masters love these guys because they are shape changers able to mimic any inanimate object. See? Not fair. They lure their prey by taking the form of helpful, desirable, or everyday objects, like doors or treasure chests, and when the unsuspecting approaches, *BAM!* They spring to life and attack. Babies in a Halloween costumes, toddlers in sports uniforms, and ten-year-olds who ask if you want to snuggle and watch holiday movies (*sigh* . . . I fall for it every time) are all Mimics. Or are they?

Oblex

Imagine if the Intellect Devourers pawned all the memories they stole from their prey to slimy, scammy telemarketers to use against innocent victims. Oblexes are those slimy, scammy telemarketers. Did you say maybe you'd go to the park on Sunday? Well, it's Sunday. So what if it's pouring and you have thirteen loads of laundry and grocery shopping to do, and a garage full of donation items you've been meaning to drop off. Approximately 156 hours ago you carelessly tossed out the idea of visiting a park, and the Oblex has come a-calling. Mean what you say or else you'll be called mean for saying it. The Oblex favors words and promises half-baked (phrases that usually start with "Maybe another time" or "In a little while" are especially delicious), while actual, realized good deeds and intentions, like that underwater ballerina pirate birthday party you pulled off in three days or how much of your income is earmarked for orthodontics, slide right off them. The more remembrances an Oblex consumes, the stronger it becomes, until it's so filled with simple musings and canceled plans, it loses all rationale. Who knew empty promises could be so filling?

Emotional Baggage of Holding

It's been said by therapists and other people much smarter than I am that you put a little bit of yourself into every D&D character—whether you realize it or not. You didn't need to cast *mirror image* to see my fears and insecurities projected on my first D&D character, Astrid Bellagio. Maybe it was because she was my first, and back when she was created it felt like it took three days to roll up a character. I didn't have time to create a new one. ("Back then" we created characters on actual paper with math, pencils, dice, and lots of eraser crumbs.) I also really loved Astrid and couldn't bear the thought of something happening to her! I didn't want to play someone else. Astrid was lovingly crafted to be everything I wanted to be: strong, magical, blond. But then the real me barged in and ruined everything.

Astrid was a young sorceress from the city of Sharn who put herself through college and graduated from the Magic Institute of Technology and Wizardry at the top of her class. She was a staunch animal rights activist who railed against her wealthy parents' fur-trading business. The family frowned upon magic users, believing they were trashy witches who lounged around in silky robes and played with orbs and flaming spheres all day. But Astrid knew she was special. She knew she had a gift and, if that gift was harnessed the right way, could help millions of animals. Probably some people too. Her family expected Astrid to finish her nonmagical studies in business and economics and join the family empire, but she longed for a life of magic and adventure! Why have these innate magical gifts if she wasn't allowed to use them? She was destined for greater things.

Then one day she got a letter from a great-aunt who affirmed what she already knew. Astrid was indeed destined for greater things! This great-aunt was also a trashy witch who lounged around in silky robes and played with orbs and flaming spheres all day. She would teach Astrid how to harness her innate magic, while housing and keeping her safe so she could study at the nearby university.

Upon graduating, Astrid was ready to put her newly honed skills to the test and joined an adventuring party called the Wyld Stallyns. She went off in search of justice, equity, and the occasional new pair of shoes. (She wasn't a saint, okay?) Although she was a badass, up-and-coming sorceress, she did more spell studying than spell-slinging badassery. Or maybe she did do cool stuff, only no one could see her do it when she was tucked behind a stone column. Did her parents get in her head? Why did she have a fanny pack full of eyeballs and mistletoe? Was this life of casting *magic missiles* from 120 feet away why she studied and worked so hard? If she had two *mage hands*, they'd be sitting there twiddling their thumbs.

While her party was ravaging aboleths and fleshrakers, she was hiding in the shrubs or cowering under the magical force of her shield. Even her party didn't count on her in combat. They told her just to stand back and take cover. What was the point? She left her morally bankrupt and fundamentally flawed family for *this*?

Oh, Astrid took damage. But it wasn't the physical kind that got to her. Astrid was beaten down by emotional damage, and no *bag of holding* could contain it all. This sweet sorcerer could carry 150 pounds but was crushed under the weight of her creator's fear and anxiety. And we're not talking about some angst-ridden god or goddess. We're talking about the person who put pencil to character sheet every Monday afternoon.

Now we all know the magic user shouldn't be the one to jump into the fray, because they're relatively unprotected (*see*: trashy witch in silky robes). All that bulky armor would only get in the way of creating beautiful orbs with your manicured fingers and toned biceps (it's my fantasy, remember?), but in those two years with the Wyld Stallyns, I'm not even sure I *played* D&D. At least not how my friends were playing it. They were threatening goblins and swinging swords and getting knocked unconscious and loving it. They required death saves! Laying on hands! Healing potions! Astrid was like the baby sister they were forced to bring along, and they knew Mom would ground them if anything happened to her. "Mom! Astrid's playing with my bow and arrow again!" I was the scared little sorceress *and* the overprotective stage mom. "You put down that *levitate* spell, young lady! You want to break your tailbone?" I was bound and determined to take the "mage" out of "damage."

Astrid made it to 7th level before the Wyld Stallyns disbanded. She was able to take a few hits here and there, and she could certainly dish it, but real-life Shelly would not let fantasy Shelly have a break. I'm not a thrill seeker in real life. I do not court danger. I won't even go on a cruise for fear of norovirus or being knocked (accidentally or on purpose) overboard. *Elderly* people aren't afraid of cruises! Elderly people are tougher than I am. If I was too paranoid to send a two-inch plastic miniature sorcerer into the world, what chance did a nineteen-inch miniature human have?

About 13 percent. That's the chance Bart and I gave our child for success, and we were definitely grading on a curve. Cleary the bulk baby prep classes didn't grant us the confidence. Even with the whole shaking the baby out of the car seat debacle, Bart was on track to be the calm, apt parent, and I was his fun but flighty sidekick. Birthday parties, school shopping, and soft skills like putting on puppet shows, writing bespoke compliments to classmates on Valentine's Day cards, and burping the alphabet fit squarely in my wheelhouse. Bart would be the go-to for the Band-Aids, tooth-pulling, and boogers part. Except, that's not how it works. Kids are like cats; they can sense the most disinterested, allergic, or ill-prepared person in the room and demand attention from that poor sap. Despite our best intentions, when our son was injured, ill, or covered in bodily fluids, his little-boy voice always called for Mama.

No one prepared me for this hamster wheel of worry, anxiety, and irrational anticipatory doom. Not a moment goes by when I'm not envisioning some awful physical or emotional damage befalling upon my sweet, innocent child. Going to a sleepover? The zipper will get stuck on his sleeping bag and he will suffocate! Playing basketball at the park? The ball will hit him in the face and he will choke on all his teeth! Watching videos about surprising animal kingdom friendships? He'll see an ad for penguin wranglers and move to the Antarctic Peninsula as soon as he's eighteen! The world is one steady stream of pitfalls and potential heartbreaks hurtling at parents and kids like rubber baseballs at carnival clown heads, and your child looks to you to shield them.

POP QUIZ!

HOW DOES SHELLY PARENT?

One time when my son was getting out of the car, I thought I slammed the door on his fingers. Did I:

A. Rush to help him

B. Realize how ridiculous that was because I was much too responsible to do something so feckless; also, he wasn't even crying

C. Spring into action with a first-aid kit, homemade tourniquet, and ambulance on the way

D. Hide behind the neighbor's garbage can, yelling "Make it stop! Make it all stop!"

If you guessed *D*, congratulations. Now you know why I don't play clerics in Dungeons & Dragons. In game, characters (except mine) get beat up, and it's part of the fun. Combat is one of the core pillars. I must reluctantly acknowledge it's also part of the *parenting* game. The game of life can be a ruthless opponent. In D&D, heroes usually have the tools to take care of themselves. Magic and mastery and healing potions help. It's kind of thrilling to take a risk when the stakes aren't real. My club D&D kids were always trying to antagonize the monsters so they'd be targeted. (Don't tell their parents.) They cheered when a monster attacked and booed if it rolled too low to hit. And when they lost hit points, they refused to rest and heal—even if it was nighttime and time to sleep, they'd ask if they could trudge on and maybe pick another fight.

"You need to close up that gaping open wound, young lady!" I yelled at the fighter. I'm a Dungeon Master, but I'm also a mom. "I know you have a healing potion!"

"Nah, I'm good," she told me. "I healed three days ago."

Then I looked at the two naughty paladins and asked them to please get some healing hands on her.

"Nope," they said. "Not without her consent."

These trash-talking kids left our D&D sessions like they were the Guardians of the Galaxy boarding their ship after the massive battle with Thanos. Walking around with 5 hit points must feel like dragging their large intestine across the four-square court. Pretty awesome! And then they returned home to homework and homemade dinners and clean pajamas in their drawers. Their world was relatively safe and secure compared to what their heroes go into for ninety minutes every week. Courting danger is fun when you know your mom is picking you up in fifteen minutes.

D&D gave them the space to feel scared and threatened within the confines of a classroom stocked with Gatorade and Goldfish crackers. These kids didn't know about *resurrection* spells or divine intervention. There were no inspirational posters at the local library proclaiming "You Only Live as Many Times as the Town Priest Is Willing to Take Your Call!" If their character bit it, they believed that's where the game ended. Maybe they'd be forced to give their spot in the club to a kid on the waitlist. Their place in our make-believe world, however ephemeral, had to have meaning. Fearing a major injury or even death did that. And yet, they kept choosing to take risks without even knowing the reward. They trusted that when they needed backup and gave their consent, the paladin would absolutely heal them.

Parenting is all meaning and matter and consequences. And it should be. It's kind of a big deal. There's a new human on this planet as the consequence of your actions. Sometimes I just look at my kid and think, *We made him! He's skin and bones and cells and he's real and no one but my mom's psychic knows what's in store for him!* An actual person who will be someone's best friend, who will break someone's heart, who will write a best-selling novel or cure a disease or look for love on a televised game show and make his mommy so proud. A human who will learn the rules, find a safe space, and look to you for healing. Even at your messiest, most anxious, most irrational self, you're still the most important person in the world to them.

Your child will get hurt, fall down, be embarrassed, get made fun of. They'll wear the wrong thing, say the wrong thing, like the wrong person. They will make mistakes. A friend will mistreat them. They will get sick, hopefully not gravely, even though you pump them up with elderberry and zinc and wash their hands until their knuckles chafe. They'll get cut from a team, lose out on the part they wanted, and be rejected from a job after six rounds of interviews. They will lose their baby teeth and get stomach bugs and wipe their runny noses on the shoulder of your last clean work shirt. And amid it all, the most magical thing of all will happen: You'll wake up every morning, slide into your mage armor, grab your shield, cast *haste*, and stand toe to toe with whatever ailment, illness, or errant kickball is heading for your child.

Even though Dungeon Masters want their players to succeed, it's not their job to remove danger from the worlds we explore. Where's the fun in that? We sit down to play together because we're excited to see where our collective imaginations will take us. DMs keep the party on their toes, challenge them, and assist in getting them to the other side so the next time danger appears (and it will), they are better equipped to deal with it. I know DMs who take it so personally when the party struggles. Was the math wrong? Did they not balance an encounter? Did they ruin D&D and now no one is having fun?

I know you *would* remove the danger from the world your child explores too, but it's not possible. What you can do is prepare them to face and overcome obstacles. Teach them resilience, empathy, and that it's okay to lean on friends and family when things get tough. Eventually, the things that kept you up at night become blips in your peripheral vision. You faced it, conquered it, bested it, or learned from it. Yes, there will always be bigger and badder threats looming in the distance, but you're bigger and badder too. And so is your adventuring party. Just as our imaginary heroes gain experience, parents will too. And they'll pass on that knowledge and confidence to their kids. There's a reason D&D has a generational appeal. Families have passed stories down to each other for centuries. Some people call them traditions. Some of us call them family game nights.

I always thought Astrid's origin story felt like that of a Disney princess. *The Trashy Little Witch*. I even wrote her a ballad.

Where the Melee Is

(Sung to the Tune of "Part of Your World" from *The Little Mermaid*)

Look at these spells,
Innate and *arcane*,
Phantasmal force and *spheres all aflame*.
Wouldn't you think I'm the mage
Who could cast anything?
I've got *ice storm* and *chill touch* and *ice knife*
Fog cloud and *cloudkill* and *false life*.
You want ranged weapons?
I've got plenty,
A critical hit when I roll a twenty.
But who cares?
I'm scared?
To die!
I wanna be where the melee is,
Fighting, blighting, hit points droppin'!
Wielding a sword with my chain mail sopping,
Slicing, dicing, but then we'll go shopping?
I mean, I'm still me inside. And I could use some new robes.

The Dice Made Me Do It

Parenting is a *transmutation* spell that turns regular, mostly happy humans into gelatinous mounds of goo. Is there any save against babies dressed in tiny hooded bathrobes designed to look like woodland creatures? No, there is not. Let's move on to something even more adorable: punishments!

Shocker: Discipline is not nearly as easy-breezy as the parents in the 1970s and '80s made it seem. They looked so happy, chasing kids around the house with a wooden spoon. It's basically how they got their steps in. (Different era, kids. Primary corrective tactics in the seventies and eighties were very, let's say, *hands on*. And not in a healing sort of way.) Another shocker: Your sweet little moochie-boochie baby bear will act out, do the wrong thing, act a fool, and require some form of correction. And ruling with a wooden spoon is generally frowned upon, so you're going to need to learn some new tactics.

There are almost as many types of discipline as there are parenting styles, and like your parenting style, you choose what's right for your family. Think of it like ordering off an à la carte menu. Choose a little from each column to create your perfect amalgamation. You may think you're one type of disciplinarian, but it's all theoretical until you're face-to-face with your little culprit. I admit, I'm pretty terrible at it. (I also untrain dogs.) I so wanted to be a tough-love mom like the one who raised me. I loved her feisty little pep talks and way she pumped me up like I was Linda Hamilton walking on the set of *The Terminator*. But the kid I got does not respond well to tough love. He doesn't even like my Yahtzee trash-talking or when I yell at the contestants on *The Bachelor*. If we raised our voices to alert him to something dangerous, like a sinkhole or our untrained dog loping toward him, he immediately thought he was in trouble and burst into tears. Sometimes we *have* to raise our voice—he gets that now— but when he's acting up, we *try* to use our normal voices and very calmly ask him to please explain what in the holy hellscape has possessed him and what we, his loving and patient caregivers, can do to remove this evil curse. (When he was very little, I convinced him I could pull a bad mood out of his ear. He must have googled it or something, because that doesn't work anymore.)

The most important thing is consistency. Experts list pros and cons to each discipline style, and no one way is considered the best for everyone or every situation, so you might have to try them all before you find one or a combination that works. What's effective for one child might not work for their sibling because—another shocker—they're all different!

There are five common forms of discipline.

Positive Discipline

This approach focuses less on punishment and more on solution-based teaching. It's described as being empathetic and kind while also being firm. Here's an example:

Matilda, a thirteen-year-old tiefling, wants to go to the market with her friends, but her moms say she has to clean the living room first. So lame! Why can't her dumb parents be petty bandits like all the other tiefling kids' parents and just leave her alone? She's clearly going to miss all the fun. Matilda's mom sits her down and says, "You know, I too was once a young child of the devil who just wanted to hang out with my friends. But it's important that you contribute to the household in a meaningful way. How can we get these rugs cleaned and fireplace swept and still get you to the market before the glove puppet flumph stall closes?"

Matilda's mom is reasoning with her by showing compassion and understanding. She restates the parents' need and offers to help find a solution to come to a compromise. Matilda's mom is practicing positive discipline!

Gentle Discipline

This style is rooted in mutual respect, redirection, and managing emotions. Similar to positive discipline, as the name may allude to, gentle discipline doesn't involve corporal punishment, but rather relies on negative consequences to course-correct and positive consequences to reward. It can also lean on humor or distraction. Let's revisit our teen tiefling Matilda and her lame parents.

Matilda, a thirteen-year-old tiefling, wants to go to the market with her friends, but her parents say she has to do the dishes first. So lame! Why can't her dumb parents be crime lords like all the other tiefling kids' parents and just leave her alone? She's clearly going to miss all the fun.

Matilda's dad sees his daughter is upset and sits her down. "Yeah, chores suck. I feel you, my little hellspawn. Would you rather wash your little brother's undergarments after we took him to that sushi restaurant in Avernus? How about you wash and I dry?"

Matilda's dad tries defusing the situation with silly humor, and once his daughter is distracted, offers help in getting the job done. Matilda's dad is practicing gentle discipline!

Boundary-Based Discipline

No surprises here. The intention is right there in the name. With this approach it's all about setting boundaries. Giving kids parameters is crucial in all aspects of parenting, not just discipline. It shows them where respectful lines are drawn and demonstrates a clear delineation when rules are not followed. Also, kids like boundaries. Contrary to how your average fourth-grader acts, they don't actually know everything and secretly want someone else to be in charge. How might Matilda respond to boundary-based discipline? Let's find out.

Matilda, a thirteen-year-old tiefling, wants to go to the market with her friends, but her parents say she has to finish the laundry. So lame! Why can't her dumb dad be a disciple of Juiblex like all the other tiefling kids' parents and just leave her alone? She's clearly going to miss all the fun! Matilda's dad is getting pretty frustrated because they keep having this conversation. "Can't you see how hard we work to keep you clothed and fed? Jeez, if we talked to our parents that way, we'd have gotten a swift tail-lashing for sure." They try a more straightforward approach: "Matilda, my dear infernal imp, if you do not wash, dry, and press the family's vests and tunics, you won't be able to visit the market for a whole month."

Harsh! But not really. Matilda has two choices. Finish her chores and meet up with her friends or ditch the chores and sulk around in dirty leggings for a month. Matilda's actions have consequences, but she is in charge of the outcome.

Behavior Modification

This one sounds like those wilderness camps the really bad kids of urban legend were carted off to in middle of the night. Thankfully, this approach is much less scary. The theory behind behavior modification is that behavior is learned and therefore can be "unlearned." Good behavior nets rewards, and bad behavior results in negative consequences. Hmm, how does Matilda respond to modifying her behavior?

Matilda, a thirteen-year-old tiefling, wants to go to the market with her friends, but her parents say she has to bathe and walk the dogs first. So lame! Why can't her dumb parents be abyssal warriors like all the other tiefling kids's parents and just leave her alone? She's clearly going to miss all the fun! *Wow, again?* Matilda's mom thinks. *If only Matlida spent as much time helping around the house as she did complaining about it, they wouldn't be on day 9 of sulfur smoothies for dinner.* Matilda's mom reminds her daughter to keep her eyes on the prize. "Don't forget, my sweet silver-eyed hellraiser, I have a 20 percent off coupon for a glove puppet, and I know how much you love flumphs. As soon as these dogs stop smelling like Zuggtmoy's mushroom palace when the AC goes out, you can head down to the market and get one."

Matilda's mom is smart to associate the negative, in this case her chores, with the positive, in this case the flumph puppet, as a means to reward the behavior she is trying to instill in her daughter.

Emotion Coaching

Think of this form as life coaching for kids. It is based on the idea that feelings and needs dictate a child's behavior and that parents must teach their kids how to express themselves in a safe and respectful way. Once a kid can articulate a feeling and talk through it, they are less likely to misdirect it by acting out. Perhaps Matilda has some misplaced feelings of anger or anxiety.

Matilda, a thirteen-year-old tiefling, wants to go to the market with her friends, but her dads say she has to help clean out the basement. So lame! Why can't her dumb dads be executing a heist in Baldur's Gate like all the other tiefling kids' parents and just leave her alone? She's clearly going to miss all the fun! *Hmm,* Matilda's father ponders. *She used to like clearing the crawl space of yochlols. I wonder what's going on with her today?* Matilda's father sympathizes with his daughter, telling her the FOMO is real and it's hard not getting to do the things you enjoy until you complete the things you dislike. Maybe she could take a break from pummeling mold spores with a mace and join him at the koi pond for a fifteen-minute meditation.

Matilda's dad validates his daughter's feelings and offers to help her find a way to process her emotions. Matilda's dad is one enlightened hellion!

Discipline is not the most fun part of parenting, but it is inevitable and inescapable. You might be surprised by which style or combination of styles you use. Dungeon Masters can at least blame the dice when something negative befalls the players. You can only blame the societal pressures of wanting to raise adaptable and emotionally well-adjusted future adults.

Building Character the Old-Fashioned Way

Kids, like D&D heroes, love treasure. And parents, like DMs, love doling it out. But there can be too much of a good thing in both cases. One of the best gifts you can give your kids is character, but it takes a lot longer to build than your D&D hero.

It's not easy denying your child something (I like to think the same is true for the DM who refused to grant me a landshark for a familiar), but sometimes it's necessary. Sure, every player character deserves a *vorpal sword*, just as every kid deserves Mr. Featherclaws, the walking, talking, plushie owlbear. But I am here to tell you: don't get it twisted. *Vorpal swords* are wasted on kids, not to mention very dangerous, so wait until they're at least eighteen (or 104 in elven years) before granting them one. And Mr. Featherclaws is bound to pass QA inspection one of these days, so feel free to add your name to the waitlist.

Knowing the difference between wanting and needing, working hard for what they want and not being an insufferable, entitled brat, aren't just great gifts for kids; they're wonderful for all of us. The good news is, the more often you say no, the easier it gets. And you'll have plenty of opportunity to practice because consumerism is an innate skill for kids.

New Dungeon Masters struggle with wanting versus needing too. Rewards are part of the game, but give the players too much, and you mess with balance and will likely have to do a bunch of math to get things back on track.

POP QUIZ!

Shelly gave the kids in her D&D club an excessive number of magic items because:

A. They thought magic items were cool
B. She wanted the kids to like D&D
C. She wasn't popular in fifth grade and really wanted a do-over
D. All of the above

Oh, fine. It's *D*. Congratulations. Now I feel obligated to give you a reward too. Perhaps inexperienced DMs are susceptible to hiding magic items in their players' backpacks to hide their lack of confidence. (They definitely are.) "Oooh, why yes, this *Mask of the Dragon Queen* would look great on you, Maya! Do you want one too, Henry?"

The kids in our D&D club had no interest in the boring old equipment on their ready-to-play character sheets. A javelin? Never heard of it. A signet ring? For what? An iron pot? Who brings an iron pot to a fight? They were much more excited to create their own weapons using the standard-issue gear in their starting equipment. One of the naughty paladins tied her signet ring to the fighter's rope and swung it around like a magic lasso. The wizard blew particles from her little bag of sand into a stirge's eye, blinding it just long enough for the rogue to duck out of the way of its attack. Before they even left for the shore of Stormwreck Isle, I had their benevolent quest-giver, Headmistress Shona, give them each a magic item. And when it became clear that not all were impressed with what they were given, I helped them find a magic-item consignment shop in town willing to trade for something cooler. The other naughty paladin got a *dagger of frost*, a magic knife that dealt an extra 1d4 of cold damage. At least that's how it was *technically* supposed to work. Under a permissive DM, it also auto-hit and rendered the opponent frozen for a turn. Oh, it could also freeze inanimate objects like trees, birds' nests, and the ground. The other paladin got an *inextinguishable candle*, which sounded exactly like one of those As-Seen-on-TV gimmicks found on an end cap at Walgreens. *Take it camping! Walk the dog! It can even go in the shower with you!* Sadly, this paladin was not in the market for perfectly pragmatic goods and snubbed it. I believe the word she used was "lame." The wizard turned her nose up at my gift of a *handy haversack*, making it seem like the equivalent of getting a bathrobe for Christmas. Even with my hard-sell skills honed from a year of working at a men's clothing store ("It has not one, but two side pouches! Each can hold up to twenty pounds! That's a lot of Jolly Ranchers!"), she still opted to trade it for a *scroll of plant growth*. The fighter had no idea what to do with a *magical vat* that, once uncorked, produced an endless flow of honey. I mean, what *couldn't* you do with an endless flow of honey? She didn't want to hurt my feelings, so she took it, but I could tell she was hoping for something more deadly and cool.

Given Miss Shelly's Permissive Pawn Shop style of Dungeon Mastering, is it any wonder these kids were all grossly overpowered and plowed through a forty-five-minute combat encounter in two and a half minutes? Now what was I going to do for the next forty-three minutes? Take them to town and give them a shopping spree with the six hundred gold pieces they were paid from their last quest? They probably didn't even know how lucky they were to have their own *deck of illusions*. I give; they take; I regret and feel guilty. And then I go home and do the same for my own kid. The cycle continues. Kids these days and their ability to turn my insecurities into a magical disguise gem.

But okay, if my worst trait as a Dungeon Master is that I spoil my players, then, guilty! I hope you take me to court and sue me for all my magic items so these kids will have to earn that *helm of brilliance* the old-fashioned way. I used to think all adventures should start at 3rd level, because that's when the fun stuff starts. A dog bite won't knock you out, and you have more options to help round out who your hero is, making all interactions in and out of combat more exciting. Really, I think I was just a lazy player. I got a taste of those higher levels and fat spellbooks, and I couldn't imagine a world in which my young wizard did not know how to cast *cloudkill*. But the 1st and 2nd levels serve a very important purpose. They're meant to be a tutorial for new players, gradually leveling up game knowledge along with their characters. It's okay to have a healthy fear of the bandits who control the ship you're trying to commandeer. Monsters *are* scary, and they eat overconfident adventurers for a midmorning snack. Heroes should struggle. Earn those gold pieces. Fail forward. Rub a little dungeon dirt on that dagger wound and get back out there. Leveling up is the equivalent of starting off in the mailroom and working your way into the C-suite.

Speaking of building character, I developed some myself thanks to a college summer spent working at Little Caesars Pizza. Not only was I forced to answer the phone with "Thank you, thank you, for calling Little Caesars Pizza, Pizza," but I spent eighty-four days reeking of peppers and sausage. Dogs would howl when I pulled into our driveway. My establishment was in a shopping plaza two doors down from the floor-covering store my dad owned, where my roommate was enjoying her cushy air-conditioned office job tapping numbers into Excel spreadsheets. She smelled like Clinique's Happy perfume.

You might be wondering why my dad didn't give *me* that cushy office job? Great question. Perhaps because back then theater majors were not taught how to use Excel, and my business-major roommate was smart enough to ask my dad for an interview and show up to it in heels and with her shirt tucked in. My dad also knew a job in food service—working with the hangry masses who all went on break at the same time and harried moms trying to feed soccer teams—would surely shore up that ol' work ethic of mine. Dad was one of my best customers, showing up at least three times a week and beaming with pride when I clipped his ticket to the order wheel and gave him back correct change. (Years later, he confessed that seeing me dressed like a sweaty traffic cone in my orange apron and wide-brimmed, unironic trucker hat made him too depressed to eat. He lost thirteen pounds that summer. I, on the other hand, gained fifteen.)

Seeing your kid struggling, perceived or real, is one of the biggest challenges for parents, even when they're engaged in perfectly normal and expected rites of passage, like dotting dough disks with circles of pepperoni. (Just so you, and especially my dad, feel better, I was offered a managerial role, but I turned it down due to my pressing theater arts studies. If only I had a sliding door to see what Assistant Manager Shelly was up to these days.) As much as I disliked that job, I made some friends and became a vegetarian shortly after I quit. The customers also provided great fodder for my sketch comedy class.

For the most part, DMs don't like seeing their players flounder either. Usually DMs have their pockets full of gold pieces and spell scrolls looking for good homes. In an informal poll of my Dungeon Mastering coworkers, one DM said seeing the party falter makes *her* feel like a failure. Clearly it was something she overlooked or miscalculated. Another said that when the players are having trouble with something and starting to get frustrated, he takes that opportunity to leave the room, pretending to get more snacks. The party uses this time to talk candidly, regroup, and regain focus, and almost always emerges victorious when they resume play.

PCs, like kids, need to earn that treasure. A dragon isn't just going to hand over its hoard, just like a quest-giver won't pay the restitution before the party accepts the mission. A pack of goblins isn't just going to be all like, "You guys look tired. We'll sit out this round so you can just take over the keep." The reward is sweeter when coupled with a little sweat equity. Other DMs agree, claiming that rewards become trivial and unmotivating when there's no healing potion the players can't buy, no weapon out of range, or no spirit they can't resurrect. Haven't you ever noticed how bored rich people look on yachts? (If not, you should definitely watch more reality TV.) What a snooze it must be to not want for a single thing.

Easier said than done? Absolutely. At this very moment my kid is begging me to take him to GameStop because a new *Pokémon* set just dropped. Does he need more *Pokémon* cards? Nope. Our Little Free Library is brimming with his discards. Do I want to make it rain buckets of booster packs because he's just the cutest, most wonderful person ever? Yes. Yes, I do. Should I tell him to dig out his piggy bank or maybe take out the garbage or walk the dog and *earn* a pack for once? What's that? Can't hear you. Must have a bad connection.

It's not all no fun and games. Your kids do deserve to have nice things and be rewarded for being the awesome extensions of you that they are. But all in moderation (says the girl who is on her way to GameStop). Admittedly, I'm still working on finding this balance, so perhaps we should let more experienced DMs take the lead.

1. **This Is Why We Can't Have Nice Things.** This lesson is brought to you from Ben and Megan, two DMs under the age of twelve. While running games for their friends, they found all sorts of joy in bequeathing the party with magic items and gold. Who wouldn't? But they also realized (unlike me) the party was becoming too overpowered. Megan hired an NPC to rob the party while they slept, taking back all of those cool high-powered magic items and most of their gold. (She basically left them enough for the Forgotten Realms equivalent of an Uber back to town.) Ben decided that all the fat loot the players were toting around was actually a mirage and made it disappear right before their eyes. Brutal, but clever.

No, I'm not suggesting you giveth just to taketh away. Or sweep their rooms while the kids are at school. We'll work on the whole magic-items-as-a-mirage tactic, but what these kids instinctually did well was course-correct. Mistakes happen. You won't even know they're mistakes until your child confronts you decades later and says their therapist is requesting a sit-down with you. But if you do notice the *ring of shooting stars* you recently gifted your child is tossed in a bin with the unsorted Lego pieces and random action-figure limbs, it might be a sign that your reward system is grossly out of whack.

2. **Minor Magic Is Still Magic.** In some games, magic items are useful—necessary, even—because the players might not survive without them. That might be a symptom of an unbalanced game rather than an extravagant Dungeon Master, says Max. It's cool to find something unique and special once in a while, but that something doesn't have to be an overpowered, turbocharged, thirty-six-months-of-a-car-payment token of appreciation. Once, my character found a mouse statue carved

out of stone and a piece of parchment with the words "When are you coming back?" Definitely not using either to barter for a *robe of the arch-magi*, but who cares? I got great ideas for my character's backstory, and everyone in the party had fun trying to figure out who was so concerned about my whereabouts.

Remember, once you go big, it's difficult to go less big. Kids have a hard time remembering to brush their teeth, but they know exactly how many gifts their sibling got for their birthday eleven months ago. There are plenty of ways to make them feel appreciated. Take them out for ice cream, get them some pizza pizza from Little Caesars, make them a coupon book granting special privileges like staying up an extra hour on a weekend night or eating breakfast in bed. You know what my kid really likes? Words of affirmation. A handwritten note saying how proud of them you are or just telling them how you noticed a cool, mature thing they did can go a long way. And it's free! Unlike all those trading cards.

3. **Play Hard, Work Hard.** Building character also builds a bank account. Say your character really wants a *masterwork sword*, but with their humble beginnings any discretionary income goes to keeping the family fed and a roof over their head. Erin is a great DM who always looks for ways to help the players achieve personal goals by making their hard work pay off, or at least *pay*. A little silver here, some gold there, maybe a grateful benefactor knows a master craftsperson who happens to owe them a favor. It's putting the "work" in "masterwork."

If you are able, giving your child a financial nudge isn't cheating or creating false expectations. It's showing them that their ideas have merit, their goal is reachable, and you believe in them. And when they finally gain enough funds to make that big purchase, they're going to appreciate it more because they know what it took to get it. My son is never more pragmatic in his purchases than when he brings his own cash to the toy store. Incidentally, those toys are the ones he takes the best care of.

4. **Eyes on the Prize.** A great philosopher by the name of Greg Tito (who also happens to be a fantastic DM) once said, "No one learns how to play basketball by reading the rulebook. You learn by watching and doing." He was talking about D&D in this reference, but it also works for parenting. Some people learn by doing, and others learn by watching. There's a reason D&D livestreams are so popular. They're

not just entertaining but also a great teaching tool. Every DM stands on the shoulders of the DMs who rolled before them. Their styles vary, offering you lots of ways to customize your own game. Dip into the way this DM introduced NPCs, try that DM's system for managing an economy, pepper in a dash of a random encounter table because they're so much fun to roll on. Still not sure where to begin? Study your friends who are parents or, better yet, their kids. Watch a whole lot of eighties sitcoms. Trust your gut. You'll not only pick up a ton of inspiration, but you'll be also doling it out in no time.

Back to those lame magic items the club kids were stuck with. Remember the night they spent on the beach? They built a sleeping hut for safety and dug a moat in the sand, filling it with honey from the *magical vat*. The *inextinguishable candle* kept the campfire burning while also providing a source of light. It kept the zombies away but attracted a family of giant guinea pigs that were also looking for shelter. Unfortunately, they got caught in the honey moat, and the sounds of their distressed squeals (some of my best voice work, thank you) woke up the party. I have yet to see this much determination and cooperation from any group I've been a party of. They spent the entire hour working together to free and tame their future mounts. And yes, Bart's group was very jealous because two giant guinea pigs were way cooler than a pet octopus. If only they had a wondrous backpack to store the four tons of groundsel and berries Butterscotch and Hibiscus ate per day. Oh wait—there's one right here! (Still working on the whole saying "no" thing.)

Is My Kid Weird?

"There is no judgier judge than an insecure parent."
—S. Mazzanoble, Very Insecure Parent

Is your kid weird? Maybe. But is that a bad thing? The best kids are the weird ones, as they're most likely to join the D&D clubs. Another great challenge for parents is not comparing your child to everyone else's.

Why is your neighbor's kid already riding a bike when your kid can barely get a spoon into their mouth? Why is your coworker at a soccer tournament every weekend when your kid doesn't even like to wear shoes? Why is a little girl in the vet's waiting room reading the same novel you just put on your wish list when your kid only likes hidden-picture books? (Because they're awesome, that's why.)

At work, my Dungeon Master ran the same adventure for two different groups of coworkers. I was in one group and my friend was in the other. He occasionally told me about how his group masterfully and cleverly handled an encounter our group biffed. I couldn't help but think, *Wow, they're so much more strategic than we are. I bet the DM loves them more than us.* But then I also heard how our mutual DM regaled the other group with tales of our autognome bard's iconic repertoire and the unlikely friendship between my plasmoid warlock and the thri-kreen ranger, both astral drifters who serendipitously found each other. He made us sound so cute.

"You guys are having so much fun," he said. "Our group is so serious."

Huh. Who knew? Everyone's a critic.

But really, *who knew?* Absolutely no one, that's who. All parents are clueless. We love our kids, but yeah—we can't help but wonder how they match up to other kids. We'll also weigh our parenting against other parents and come up short almost every time. (I like to watch the occasional Lifetime movie to make myself feel better about my mom proficiency.) But get this: Someone is comparing themself to you right now and wishing they could be half as confident and capable as you are. I'm onto it, but it took years to figure out. We're all just one Mayo Clinic article away from crumbling under our own inferiority. Not one parent isn't worried about who their child is or will become. There is no perfect kid. They're all struggling with something. That kid who's great at hockey refuses to eat anything except ketchup and potato chips. That kid who won the global reading challenge gets violently motion sick if they spend more than three minutes in a car. The kid who plays three musical instruments and goes to an artsy summer camp *for a month* every summer yells at the teacher and once hit a classmate in the face with a broom. So yeah, no one's perfect. Not even close.

I have a coffee mug that proudly proclaims "Not the worst mom!" I gifted it to myself. It serves as a nice reminder that I am not, in fact, the worst mom, and wow, what a relief that is. I also have quite a few mugs that declare me to be the best mom, so who knows? Like art, parenting is subjective. You're doing great. To someone else, at least.

Tears of Play

As your D&D character levels up, the world in which they interact grows alongside them. These are known as the tiers of play. Once completed, a new set of challenges and events is introduced, gradually increasing in difficulty. Each tier lists ideal milestones players will encounter and resolve as they move on up in their adventuring careers. *Ideal* milestones. Keep that in mind.

Kids also hit multiple milestones as they move through the various developmental stages—sometimes it seems like all in one day. You might feel like your kid will never leave the thumb-sucking, beige-food, challenge-everything-you-say phase, and in the blink of an eye you're helping them buy sheets for their new apartment. These parenting milestones are called "tears of play." You wouldn't have a 1st level character face off against a tarrasque, just as you won't let a baby drive a car. You, as the caregiver, create a safe and nurturing space for your baby to gradually learn basic skills, like holding a fork and pointing to their shoes.

It might seem like your DM is firing off a constant stream of big bads at the party, but there actually is a method to their madness. Just like how a personal trainer slowly increases the weight on their client's seated leg presses, they're not doing it to make you feel inferior and inadequate so you'll keep paying them to make you swole. Quite the contrary. They're doing it because they're good at their job. You're getting stronger, and they must keep challenging you.

Parents and DMs adapt to their changing charges too. The only difference is that in D&D the Dungeon Master controls the environment and those who inhabit it. The real world? Well, that's controlled by the real world. One of my biggest fears as a parent is thinking I'm not doing enough to prepare my son for the big bads he will inevitably face along his journey. But rest assured, by appropriately scaling their training like a Dungeon Master, your little adventurers will be sending you postcards from the farthest reaches of the multiverse in no time. Here's how to manage milestones using the tears of play.

Little Heroes

AGES 0–4

Levels 1–4

Welcome to the world, tiny adventurers!

A fledgling character is full of hope and promise and the thrill of adventure. At this stage they are figuring out how to be them, whether that's a dwarf cleric or a brand-new human. Parents and Dungeon Masters are key influencers in this phase, as most new humans and characters practice mimicking the behaviors they see in others.

HOW THEIR WORLDS COMPARE

D&D Hero	Real-World Hero
Figuring out how their chosen class defines them and how to use new skills	Figuring out how a Thomas the Tank Engine T-shirt defines them and how to use their hands
Magic items consist of common consumables like brews, scrolls, and potions	Food items consist of liquids, pouches, and rice husks; some of these are also considered "magic items"
Uses mostly mundane gear and weapons	Uses mostly organic and nontoxic gear; favors improvised weapons
Revered by small towns and local innkeepers	Revered by parents, grandparents, friends of parents, and cashiers
Prefers to hang out in haunted crypts, dungeons, and keeps	Prefers to hang out in doorway jumpers, parks, and bathtubs
Often foiled by powerful monsters, unbalanced encounters, and impatience	Often foiled by naptime, imbalance, hanger, and impatience

Heroes of the Playground

AGES 5–10

Levels 5–10

At this stage both fantasy and real-life heroes have had some time to learn basic life skills and put this new understanding into practice. There is a lot of learning in this phase—much of which will become the foundation for who both sets of heroes will become.

A D&D hero has a solid, fleshed-out identity; becomes a legit threat in combat thanks to a fair amount of hit points and abilities; and gains proficiency with armor and weapons, as well as a new subclass. The real-world hero might find themself gaining invaluable academic and social-emotional training thanks to starting school. As their thirst for knowledge ramps up, beloved board books are replaced with word searches and mazes, and analytical and problem-solving skills are built by an insatiable curiosity usually in the form of questions that begin with "Why".

Both heroes grow physically stronger in this phase as well. They hone motor skills and gain muscle coordination in preparation for mastering two-weapon fighting and the buttons on a jacket or a game controller.

HOW THEIR WORLDS COMPARE

D&D Hero	Real-World Hero
Asks a lot of questions about the setting, lore, and rules	Asks a lot of questions
Very loyal to their party, patron, or pact	Not loyal; tries on alliances like they are *PAW Patrol* underwear on potty-training day, but can blow them up just as quickly
Heavily influenced by bonds, ideals, and flaws	Heavily influenced by friends, advertising, and content creators
Feels confident in the world and resolute in their role in protecting it	Feels confident in the world one minute, alienated the next, but resolute in their quest to protect their planet

HOW THEIR WORLDS COMPARE (continued)

D&D Hero	Real-World Hero
Weapons, armor, and spells become more impactful and useful	Toys and clothing become louder, more complex, and more expensive
Enjoys meeting locals and the company of a diverse cast of characters from across the realms	Enjoys meeting other kids similar in age, unless there's a popular toy, snack, or suspected video game cheating scandal

Masters of the Awkward

AGES 11–17

Levels 11–16

Congratulations, parents! You are no longer needed—at least according to your offspring, who has now figured out every fact, facet, and fold of the universe. It's liberating! Go take a long bath.

D&D heroes at this level are highly regarded. Their real-world counterparts certainly believe they are as well. These adventurers have paid their dues, have licked their wounds, and have the tall tales to prove it. They're powerful and respected, courageous and tenacious, resourceful and influential. I once played a one-shot as an 11th level character and found myself so overwhelmed by my awesomeness, I kept using the same two spells and didn't do anything awesome. Lame! (I guess that's why we're supposed to gradually level up.)

Kids at this age enter the dreaded tween and teen years. It's as troubling and awkward as you remember it. Imagine if you were a DM and the party chose completely new characters every week. That's what it's like to parent a teenager.

HOW THEIR WORLDS COMPARE

D&D Hero	Real-World Hero
Begins to think about long-term plans, including retirement	Begins to think about long-term plans, including what they'll do that night
Spends time thinking about the role they played in society and where their statue will be erected	Spends time thinking about the role they'll play in society and who they want to be their roommate
Has recovered many lost artifacts for powerful benefactors	Has not managed to recover one baseball jersey for the game starting in 8 minutes
Enjoys being regaled with songs about their heroic deeds	Enjoys being regaled with song parodies about their favorite video games, memes, and farts
Will leave their mark on the world in the form of guilds, temples, and reputation	Will leave their disgusting mark on anything in the form of a hole through the drywall, stains on the couch, or a big dent in your retirement fund
Increased interest in negotiating a higher fee in exchange for thwarting a nefarious plan or stopping a war	Increased interest in debating social justice and world political topics and also a higher fee in allowance because they have to do everything and it's so unfair

Masters of the Open World

AGES 18–21

Levels 17–20

At this stage, what is left for a D&D hero to do? They've seen and done it all. Their exploits are all but the stuff of legend. Mere mortals can only dare to dream of attaining even a fraction of their heroism. A level 20 character is almost godlike.

While Masters of the D&D world may be winding down their adventuring career and living off the residuals of their own legend, your master of the open world is ripping off the protective film, taking that diploma or first job, and embarking on their first solo adventure.

HOW THEIR WORLDS COMPARE

D&D Hero	Real-World Hero
May ascend to the heavens to serve a god or discover the key to life everlasting	May depart for college or begin learning a trade or working in their chosen field
Has acquired a collection of high-powered rare magic items	Has acquired a collection of mismatched secondhand furniture, extracurricular trophies and medals, and possibly debilitating student debt
Is a well-known super-heroic adventurer with an extensive library of songs honoring their legendary career, foundations built to continue their good works, and iconic namesake spells	Begins to establish themself as an independent person with distinct likes, dislikes, personal philosophies, and preferences
Has a remarkably high tolerance for death	Has a remarkably high tolerance
Can summon and ride a mystical beast	Can summon a ride thanks to an app
Will traverse other realms and extraplanar destinations in search of archmages, demons, power, and riches	Will traverse other continents in search of popular attractions, cheap eats, and a study abroad semester

Remember, it's not about the destination; it's about all the heroic things your tiny adventurer will do along the journey. How will you know they'll be successful? Because you've walked alongside them every step of the way, ensuring the hero will surpass the master.

What's Left of the Ruins

The dad of one of my club kids told me how much fun his daughter was having playing D&D. An avid fan himself since the eighties, this no doubt delighted him. I told him how great it must be to bond with his daughter over their shared love of Dungeons & Dragons. Bet he never thought about this moment when he was ten years old, hiding his copy of *Deities & Demigods* between his mattress and box spring like it was freshly laundered money.

"Well, I'm forbidden from talking about it," he said. *"At all."*

Uh-oh. His daughter was a great wizard and did something funny and remarkable every session. Why wouldn't he talk about it?

"Because if she knew how excited I was, she'd immediately stop playing D&D. No way am I going to ruin this!"

Yep. I could relate.

"Well," I said, "I ruined baseball, *The Goonies*, and Christmas decorating."

"I ruined Legos and Ultimate Frisbee, and I have to be careful with skiing," the dad continued. "If I stay quiet about D&D, she'll think she discovered it and maybe invite me to play."

There's a fine line between passing on your fandom and being a complete and utter loser who likes dumb, losery things. *Never show your hand!* Especially if it's a hand filled with the Judy Blume books you read as a child and your first edition *Dungeon Master's Guide.* You must practice feigning interest, even sort of brushing them off and fostering a healthy scent of elitism. Nothing piques a kid's appetite like being told they can't have something. It's more studied and complicated than a capoeira dance.

I could feel myself dancing dangerously close to the creative writing ruins as well. Lately my son has shown interest in writing (very) short stories, and while they're not quite up to the erudite disquisition you're reading now, it's because he hasn't learned how to use a thesaurus yet. I hate admitting this, but perhaps my biggest failure as a parent is ruining (or co-ruining, because Bart gets credit here too) Dungeons & Dragons. My son . . . doesn't want to play.

It's my fault. I came on too strong. Wanted it too much. He could sense my hunger. I made a wild assumption that a game about making up stories and casting spells and being told "Yes, you can do that!" would appeal to a kid. Especially a game that involved cool accessories and snacks. My bad! The only saving grace I had was that his friends were discovering D&D on their own and asking for *Player's Handbooks* and spell cards for their birthdays. Not all peer pressure is bad. Several of his friends were on the waitlist for our D&D club. The very club my son was forced to join because we didn't have anyone to watch him while we played D&D with his classmates. He spent the time reading in the hallway or distracting his friends, only returning to his seat when it was his turn in combat.

It's only natural to want your children to love the things that also bring or brought you joy. Why shouldn't visiting seven different TJ Maxxes on a Saturday afternoon in search of matte black flatware be as exciting for him as it is for me? Would his first words be "Mama, will you accept this rose?" How thrilling would it be to pull out the Christmas decorations from the garage in early November? (I would start sooner, but I need a full week to de-Halloween the house.) We start with a winter woodland creatures theme. Think squirrels in flannel scarves and snowy-white bottle-brush owls infiltrating the bookshelves. Chubby cardinals in plaid vests and foxes with sleds continue popping up on bookshelves and windowsills and on dishtowels and throw pillows. The week before Thanksgiving, it's a full-on Christmas assault. We're talking bathmats, shower curtains, comforters, blankets, dog bowls, and coffee mugs, all victims of the Christmas ambush glow-up. If anything stays in one place long enough, it will be covered with garland, a wreath, or strings of colorful fairy lights. (Sometimes all three.) I hired an electrician to install two additional outdoor outlets so I could execute my "vision" without tripping a fuse. What kid doesn't get excited about living inside of a snow globe and coming home from school, slipping on a festive apron, and spending the next three hours baking sugar cookies and peppermint thumbprints? Who in their right mind leaves the room two and a half minutes into *Emmet Otter's Jug-Band Christmas* claiming it's "too old-fashioned" and "boring"? It's got *otters* and *Christmas*! What's not to love?

Now, my son loves Christmas as an occasion. He's somewhat proud when his friends ask their parents to drive by our house, affectionately referred to as Little Las Vegas (which may also be because I serve up a mean brunch and taught my son basic math by playing blackjack.) But other than one adorable and disgusting time when he was three years old and decorated our Christmas tree with slices of deli ham, he's more of an *observer* to the process. I can't tell you how many ramshackle gingerbread houses he's left in his apathetic path.

Bart was buying vintage Star Wars action figures before we even decided to have a child. In Bart's mind, seeing his child playing with the same toys he did was peak dad fulfillment. Admittedly, said child has more of an appreciation for four-inch army men with five points of articulation than he does for discount home goods or chubby cardinals in dapper cold-weather gear, but his Star Wars fandom peaked and fizzled by age five.

"What did I do wrong?" Bart pondered while replacing a vintage C-3PO bedspread with a brand new one featuring Peely, the smartly dressed banana guy from *Fortnite*.

"You wanted it too much," I said. "We are pushy and sad humans. Just disgusting."

There weren't enough C-3PO blankets in the world to warm the coldness that seeped into Bart's fandom-obsessed heart. But we only had ourselves to blame. From a very young age, kids can sniff out and turn on an overeager sales pitch. No, shots are not fun, even when you stop for ice cream on the way home. Math problems have the word "problems" baked right in there! We were merely incarnations of Willy Loman, peddling our childhood wares, sad, weary, and desperate for our progeny's affirmation of the things that made us whole.

Then this very strange phenomenon happens when you're too busy reading Sweet Valley High books by yourself. Your kids grow up. They get more independent, becoming self-sufficient and bossy. Their clothes slide off the tiny baby hangers their toddler clothes used to hang on. They watch live-action TV shows instead of cartoons. They start forming *opinions*. So many opinions. They want to dress themselves and spend more time with friends, and they're less portable. They want their own alarm clock, and they learn how to use microwaves and tea kettles to make their own ramen. And best of all, they develop interests—their own interests—which in turn become yours. I couldn't stand the sound of squeaky sneakers on a sweaty court, but now I spend several nights a week cheering on the Golden State Warriors from our couch. I'm also very well-versed in basketball trivia and know six different terms for making a basket. Since becoming a mom, I've grown proficient in *Fortnite* dances, different types of Pokémon, and graphic novels. I can still name all of Thomas the Tank Engine's friends. It's cool to see them transform from your sentient Tamagotchi into a full-fledged human.

But fear not. It's not goodbye. It's not even "see ya later." Watching your kids grow into their own personalities is like using a random character generator. Maybe they have your eyes and delicate ankles but are agile and athletic. Maybe they're an avid reader but don't think *Tales of a Fourth Grade Nothing* is the literary marvel you grew up thinking it was. Maybe somewhere in your lineage there was a mathematician and a scientist whose brainy ancestry is flooding your child's veins.

As all Dungeon Masters know, players gotta play. They create the sandbox so adventurers can explore it. They go left when you think they'll go right. They reject the quest in favor of trying out all the local restaurants in town. They fall in love with a throwaway NPC whose sole purpose was to offer them lodging for the night and invite them to join the party. They were built for this stuff. It's all "Yes, and . . ." this and "Yes, and . . ." that. They don't just roll with the punches; they roll the dice that determine where those punches land. They love watching characters develop and stories unfold almost as much as the players do. They don't just brace for the unexpected; they embrace the unexpected. It's one of the best lessons Dungeon Masters can teach us parents.

I always describe the Dungeon Master as the narrator, but maybe they're more like the on-call support system there to answer questions and make sure nothing—especially the players—breaks. Dungeons & Dragons is a cooperative storytelling game, and within all those narrative threads, there are individual stories that evolve and expand and shift and surprise, and they almost always intersect and create new stories. I love watching my son become his own little human with his own interests and passions, and I'm starting to embrace the element of surprise too. Who will he be today? Who will he become tomorrow? Will he be happy? Because that's the important thing, right? Maybe kids these days can't appreciate the beautiful story of the sacrifices a widowed otter mother made for her son, Emmet, at Christmastime, but they will appreciate their own parents for introducing them to a world full of interesting and wonderful delights their own kids will reject one day. Don't worry, they never forget their first Dungeon Master.

Changelings in the Air

You can't change your child's budding interests to match your own, but something *will* change: you. I know you're probably thinking, *Of course I changed! I'm a parent now! I volunteer in classrooms and host birthday parties for six-year-olds.* True, true, but the change is much more fundamental than that.

And it should be. Despite what I thought I knew about myself, it turns out I will share my dessert with my son. You have no idea how much *PJ Masks* you can withstand until you're literally singing the theme song during a work meeting. I will cram myself into a tiny toddler bed, rubbing my son's back until he falls back asleep. You can't fight it. Parenting is like its own subclass. You're going to gain all sorts of cool new skills.

- **Using your toes as fingers.** Sometimes that thing you need is just out of reach and a baby is asleep in the crook of your arm. Getting dexterous with your southernmost phalanges is the next best thing to a *mage hand*.
- **Catching up on sleep anywhere, anytime.** Son's out, pass out. "Sleep when the baby sleeps" is good advice, and sometimes you won't be able to help it. Like our elven counterparts, a little trance-out session goes a long way.
- **Polymorphing into your parents.** Yes, I've heard my mom's voice saying my mom's words from my own mouth. What sorcery is that? You too will have the ability to not just turn into your parents but really any parent whose work you admire. You will also gain a mom or dad voice around the time your child turns one, granting you +5 to all commands.
- **Caring deeply about things you didn't even know were things people cared about.** You will become an expert in construction trucks, the art of making slime, and on-base percentages for nine-year-old baseball players. The student-to-teacher ratio of your public school system will get you really fired up.
- **Making sacrifices (and not the obvious ones!).** I thought laying off the malbec for forty weeks was the ultimate sacrifice, and yet there is no end to what you are capable of doing to support your kid. You will wake

up before bakers have their first buns in the oven, give up hockey playoff tickets in favor of *Daniel Tiger Live*, and dip well into your custom game-table reserve to fund your little baller's summer basketball camp dreams.

But the most surprising part? You won't just do these things; you'll *love* doing these things. You're like a kind, benevolent patron to an adorable, manipulative warlock. Change is good.

Moppet Manual: Lurking Ooze

The Lurking Ooze is the embodiment of a bark that's worse than the bite. Don't get it twisted, though: they'll bite—with words and actions—and they are rabid. Lurking Oozes appear like specters, haunting the very locations and people they used to favor. They take over the minds of younger, smaller beings like the Bewitched Betwixts, offering the occasional glimmer of the sweet fallen angels they once were.

Lurking Oozes are in the throes of newly found independence, caught between wanting to do all the things and having no resources to act upon those wants. They are rash and impetuous, and if they can muster the energy to do so, they are prone to poor choices or act inappropriately. Expect a Lurking Ooze to display no remorse or ownership for their actions. They spend as much time as possible away from their homes, only returning when they need food, money, or clean clothes.

Seldom seen alone in the wild, when one Lurking Ooze is spotted, you can count on their pack being close by. They can be tracked by their scent—usually a tangy-pork-rind-and-amaretto fragrance. Lurking Oozes enjoy taking up space, preferably spreading out across shop entrances even though they have no intention of patronizing those shops or flowing across a busy urban sidewalk. The mere presence of a group of Lurking Oozes instills fear in their opponents, often leaving them petrified and exhausted. Lurking Oozes are vulnerable to sunlight and prefer to stay indoors until twilight. They sleep fourteen hours a day.

Lurking Oozes have an insatiable appetite and can pack away several tons of food each day. Their families can't stand them but also miss them when they are not around. When Lurking Oozes grow up and leave the nest, they will return, calmer and more loving, to their homes and families, who welcome them with open arms.

➤ **Best Defense:** *Just leave them alone!*

LURKING OOZE

Huge, typically (and hopefully temporarily) Chaotic Evil

Armor Class 16
Hit Points 32
Speed Whenever they get there! Stop rushing them!

STR	DEX	CON	INT	WIS	CHA
14	11	12	10	11	8

Skills Deception +8, Stealth +5, Sleight of Hand +6
Damage Resistances poison
Damage Immunities cold, psychic
Condition Immunities petrified, deafened, guilted
Challenge 16 (56,000 XP)

Eye Roll. The Lurking Ooze can roll its eyes all the way back into its head, causing each creature within 120 feet to make a DC 18 Intelligence saving throw or become as embarrassing as they think you are.

Advanced Telepathy. The Lurking Ooze can magically transmit simple messages and coded symbols to other Lurking Ooze anywhere in the world if in possession of a Sending Stone device. Should this form of telepathy be intercepted by anyone other than a Lurking Ooze, the messages will be indecipherable and drive the reader to certain madness and paranoia.

You Don't Get It. The Lurking Ooze can communicate with other creatures using a common language, but you won't get it because you are being sus and have probably already been afflicted with *cringe*.

ACTIONS

Tongue Lashing. Lurking Ooze have auto-hit on attacks below the belt. Each target must succeed on a Wisdom saving throw or take 2d6 psychic damage and have disadvantage until the Lurking Ooze either apologizes or moves out of your house.

Leave Me Alone! Lurking Ooze can retreat within themselves, gaining +5 to their armor class until it emerges.

Cringe. Lurking Ooze can cast *cringe* on unsuspecting creatures going about their normal business. When *cringe* is cast, each afflicted creature is labeled as such and takes 1d4 psychic damage. There is no save against being called *cringe*, and it's near impossible to recover from.

We Never Left the Tavern

I like a good plot twist as much as anyone, but not even the most seasoned Dungeon Master could anticipate the giant bombshell turn of events March 2020 brought us. If a "Great Pandemic" happened in a game, I would have thought it was too contrived and unfathomable—even for a fantasy world. "Really? A plague rips through a plane of existence, and only us heroes can stop it? Snooze. Heard that one before. We didn't come all this way just to stay at the inn."

Silver lining? More time to play! As the world was shutting down, games were starting up. People around the world were discovering or rediscovering D&D as a means to stay connected in our ever-shrinking world. And those who were already playing were not willing to let their gaming group go and thus found a multitude of ways to play together online. There were only so many Zoom happy hours and online trivia tournaments we could handle. D&D always had a new story to tell, as often as you wanted. We didn't leave our homes, but we explored fallen temples and ancient ruins. We apprenticed for powerful mages and martial artists. We attuned to powerful magic items and unearthed lost artifacts. We bonded with our party, even when they were thousands of miles away.

A global pandemic is basically one long session zero. My kid was one of many who fell behind in school and had way too much screen time. I spent my first ever Christmas without my immediate family. Our basement flooded, and we couldn't turn on our Christmas lights without tripping a fuse thanks to the giant industrial fans sucking all the moisture out of our environment. We lost loved ones before we had a chance to say goodbye. I gained twenty pounds, even with all the pacing around I did like an anxious, restless panther. But I also read a lot of books and took walks and listened to podcasts and got on the home-made-bread bandwagon (hello, twenty pounds!). I even noticed the adorable spray of freckles across the bridge of my son's nose. How long had those been there? While I hated the collective grief and panic and global divide caused by the pandemic, I am grateful for the quality time I got with my son, husband, cat, and dog, as well as the bevy of foster dogs we welcomed. If we can make it through COVID, puberty should be a breeze, right?

I'm not trained in survival, and I'm certainly not wishing for the world to shut down again, but should you find yourself with considerable time on your hands and a need to stay busy, take a cue from how your D&D character would handle downtime.

Downtime in D&D is the period of time between adventures when the characters rest, prepare for their next quest, or practice new skills and hobbies. Some Dungeon Masters may handwave the passage of time, but others use this time to work on their side hustles. Here are some recommended ways you and your character could be spending your downtime.

Recuperating, aka "Practicing Self-Care"

When taking a short rest, your character's idea of self-care might mean "tending to wounds." You can do better. Personally, I'm annoyed by the modern-day definition of self-care because it makes it sound like doing basic human functions is somehow above-and-beyond pampering. I mean, showering is rudimentary, and while it can feel refreshing, it shouldn't be looked at as an indulgence. But when it's a long bath? With essential oils and Epsom salts? The luxury! Taking a walk without a destination, just to enjoy the outdoors? You heathen! Cooking a three-course meal from scratch? And eating it? Total debauchery! Take the time to do the things you enjoy—without the guilt! You deserve it!

Crafting, aka "Enjoying Hobbies"

As a new parent, you might feel like your new caregiver identity negates the old you. But get this: If you liked sports before becoming a mom, you'll still like sports after. If you enjoyed gardening before you were someone's dad, good news—you are still the neighborhood biodynamic soil expert. Just as a well-rounded party is key to the player's success, your kid gets to reap all that inherent knowledge from their cultivated parents. They'll become masters of the elástico move and can list the pros and cons of succession planting versus companion planting. More important, they'll see their parents independently finding joy in pastimes. Kids mimic behaviors they see in the home, so you go ahead and read a book.

Practicing a Profession, aka "Getting a Job"

Yes, yes, we know parenthood is the most important job we'll ever have, but it's not the only one. Sometimes your D&D character might take jobs between adventures (which sounds like the opposite of downtime, but you do you!). If they're proficient in performance, they can put those skills to use and lead a wealthy lifestyle (which, speaking as a former theater major, sounds the most like a fantasy). The human you can net a part-time gig, monetize a side hustle, or volunteer your time for a cause important to you. It's a great reason to get out of the house and spend time with other adults.

Carousing, aka "Hanging Out with Friends"

In between adventures your heroic self likes to kick back in a tavern, knocking back a few drinks and retelling tales about their most recent hard-fought quest. Sounds delightful. As Kevin Bacon once said, "I gotta cut loose," and so do parents. Despite that tiny human always fourteen inches away, raising children can be lonely and isolating. Social connection is a must.

Recuperating, aka "Recuperating"

This one needs no explanation. You must take care of yourself and find additional support. Join a group, talk to a friend, or just enjoy some rare time alone. Your physical and mental health will take a beating as a new parent. Nearly 20 percent of women will experience postpartum anxiety or depression, and those are just the cases that are diagnosed. Some amount of baby blues or nervousness is expected, but if you think you need professional help, trust your instincts (and not some stupid survey you found online) and get help.

Researching, aka "Mastering the Art of Me Time"

Your D&D character might use this time to tuck into a library, poring over a dusty tome in search of clues leading to an ancient mystery. In real life you might be digging into a juicy tell-all about the cultish and corrupt beauty industry (I have recs) or holed up in the backyard honing your cornhole skills. (Hey, there's still a chance you could go pro!) Researching means different things to different people. I like to think of it as investigating your own personal history. What *did* you like to do when you had copious amounts of free time? Oh, right! Do that.

Training, aka "Sharpening a New or Existing Skill"

I know what you're thinking: *Who has the time or energy to master a new skill when you are still perfecting how to purée boiled peas into an appetizing paste?* Your D&D character is also busy with a full-time adventuring job, yet as soon as they get a little time off between gigs, they're out there learning a new language or perfecting another fighting style. Nerds! You don't have to squeeze into a gi to treat your cerebral cortex to a delicious treat. Do an online yoga or stretching class (there are tons of free videos). Take a virtual cooking class. Sign up for those Spanish lessons you've been putting off. Knowledge is power, and you'll need all that mental brawn to remember the words to your child's favorite book when you inevitably leave it behind.

Epilogue: The Quest Continues

(Because It Never Ends. You Know That, Right?
This Is Your Life Forever.)

There you are, at the mouth of a cave, deep in the belly of the Underdark. The party winds their way through dank dungeons filled with stalagmites and stalactites (and people who still don't know the difference) in search of clues and relics and oft-revered treasure. *There's nothing here*, you think. *Maybe we should turn back.* But you won't. You trudge forth, the promise of what lies ahead too irresistible to quell.

Then you see a glimmer of something—a few silver pieces or a gem encrusted with centuries of muck and mud. Perhaps it was dislodged and discarded from something much more valuable. Maybe that something is still down here. You put the gem in your pouch and keep moving forward, heady with hope. Something big is coming your way. You can feel it. This is why you put on your armor, pick up your shield, and risk your life running headfirst into the unknown every single time. The hint of promise is what keeps you going. So off you go to the next dungeon and the next and the next, picking up small treasures along the way. Some have monetary value; some have emotional worth. Some you work hard for, only to discover they're worthless. As you come to what you presume is the last dungeon, you are momentarily disappointed. *Nothing!* Someone must have gotten to it first. You drop to your knees under the weight of unfulfilled anticipation. Or maybe it's the heft of a rucksack brimming with riches. Where did all this treasure come from? Some of it you don't even remember picking up. Most of it doesn't have value, but it's worth everything to you.

That's when you realize the treasure doesn't come at the end. There is no end. The real reward is in the journey and the accumulation of memories you picked up along the way. You'll never stop fighting the bad guys, never stop trying to save a town, never stop checking for traps so less-experienced adventurers can have safe passage.

I found a quote from self-help author Beth Kempton that's been my refrain since I started writing this book. She said, "I don't write books because I have all the answers. I write books because I have so many questions." Every day of parenthood begets baffling new questions. I don't have the answers. (Sorry, should I have told you that sooner?) Or at least, *your* answers. It's different for all of us. Families are different. Just like in D&D, there is no perfect party. A fighter, a wizard, a rogue, and a cleric do not guarantee success. I once played in a party of all rogues and we were very effective (and very quiet). Maybe you're in the throes of it, maybe you haven't even started yet, maybe your little heroes are about to split the party and go off on their own. You could probably write your own book about parenting, and I wish you would, so we can compare notes and realize there's no right way to do it. Just like a D&D adventure unfolds before the players, so will your parenting journey. It may feel like you are ill prepared or stuck at 1st level, or maybe you're still trying to get your game scheduled, but somehow, someway, you will figure it out and come out the other side, bigger, tougher, and richer. (Figuratively, of course. Unless you become a stage parent, and then good luck. I look forward to reading your child's future memoir.)

I learned a lot about raising kids from Dungeons & Dragons, but oddly enough I also learned a lot about parenting from playing D&D with kids, especially this: stop caring so much. Yes, I know it's weird to tell you to stop caring so much when it comes to your children, but it's the "so much" part I want you to remember. If the kids in my D&D club wanted to make their own weapons or skip the Sea Caves to spend the night injured and unprotected on a zombie-infested beach, *Why should I care so much?* They had their best session that day. We still talk about Butterscotch and Hibiscus a year later. There is so much real stuff to worry about (sorry), you'll actually be doing yourself a favor to let the little things go. I tell myself several times a day, *Nah, that's too much.* No one cares if your kid comes home early from a sleepover. Your six-year-old not trying sashimi doesn't preclude them from getting into college one day. Amazing things happen when you stop caring so much. Kids develop without fear of failure or causing disappointment. They grow up to be self-assured, confident adults. You won't get any credit for that, but we know the truth.

I am not the mother I thought I would be. I'm better. Phew! Thank goodness. But yeah, the bar was pretty low. Do I sometimes fantasize about my single days living alone in a condo eating a can of beans for dinner and watching episodes of *House Hunters* I recorded on my TiVo until I fell asleep on my couch? Oh yes! Do I think a woman who once sustained herself on a can of beans should be in charge of another person? Questionable. Is being someone's mom the most scary, astonishing, mind-blowing, emotionally draining, mentally fulfilling, anxiety-ridden, eye-opening, fun thing I never did? Absolutely. They say parenting is a "job," but it doesn't feel like a job when you're doing what you love. Also, you don't get paid.

If you're worried about what kind of parent you'll be, you're already ahead of the game. You're exactly who should be out there raising the next generation of adventurers. And if you're a Dungeon Master, you're not just ahead of the game; you *are* the game. It was in you all along!

I'll leave you here (pretend it's a tavern), but in no way is this the end of your story. In a game of Dungeons & Dragons you can be a Dungeon Master or you can be a hero. In parenting, you're lucky because you get to be both.

Acknowledgments

I am eternally grateful to be surrounded by the most epic adventuring party who has kicked down doors, fought ferocious beasts, and crushed Charisma checks while I hung out with my familiar, working on this spellbook.

The University of Iowa Press is a critical hit across the board. Thank you, Meredith Stabel, for saying yes to a second book. I am blessed to be guided by your wisdom, insight, and intelligence (see what I did there?). Thank you to Danielle Johnsen, Kat Reagan, Allison Means, Susan Hill Newton, Maya Torrez, and everyone at University of Iowa Press who has shared an idea or an opinion and helped this little book level up along the way. It is an honor to work with you all again!

Enormous gratitude and apologies to Lori Paximadis. Copyeditors are the unsung heroes in the publishing world and must be protected at all costs. (Sorry, still don't know what to do with a comma.) And thank you to proofreader Alisha Jeddeloh. And many thanks to Tanya DePass for your nat 20 Perception. You are an inspiration as always.

Many thanks to the Wizards in the party—my coworkers and friends—who taught me so much about Dungeon Masters and Dungeon Mastering. Extra gratitude to Lindsey Quintana and Layla Maurer for clearing the way, and to Liz Schuh—still my most favorite wizard—for endless support and agreeing to *another* D&D book. Who knew forcing me to play D&D all those years ago would lead to this?

So much gratitude to Saritza Hernandez for being my party's fighter, relentless champion, door-kicker-downer, and Disney concierge. This is a campaign, not a one-shot. There are so many more adventures to come!

I would be lost in a dungeon without food rations or a light source if not for my emotional support clerics. Thank you, Erin Hawes and Kari Murphy, for the nonjudgmental driveway chats, laughs, and unwavering support. Thank you also for trusting me to take your amazing kids on weekly adventures and write about it (and only sometimes remembering to change their names). Much gratitude to the fearless friends Desiree Jordan, Nina Hess, Kristina Koser, and Kristina "Gorla" Morello, who braved this whole mom thing well before me and are giving me all the secrets to raising awesome kids.

To my dad, who taught me a thing or two, and to my mom for teaching me everything else. And to my brother, Mike, because for us pseudo-latchkey kids of the eighties, your older brother is basically a parent, right?

To Bart, vanquisher of evil, doer of good, occasional topper of bookshelves, and calmer of harpies. There is no one I'd rather be on this adventure with.

To Quinn. What can I say? You are the most epic of quests, the grandest of adventures, and the richest reward. Even though I fancy myself a sorcerer, I'll always be a fighter when it comes to you.

And to all the parents reading this: I grant you inspiration and advantage on all your dice rolls forever and ever. I have the power to do so, right? I'm a Dungeon Master!